IT ALL BEGAN WITH
WILT

IT ALL BEGAN WITH

WILT

By Wilt Chamberlain's
High School Coach

CECIL MOSENSON

TATE PUBLISHING & *Enterprises*

Published by Tate Publishing & Enterprises, LLC
127 E. Trade Center Terrace | Mustang, Oklahoma 73064 USA
1.888.361.9473 | www.tatepublishing.com

Tate Publishing is committed to excellence in the publishing industry. The company reflects the philosophy established by the founders, based on Psalm 68:11,
"The Lord gave the word and great was the company of those who published it."

Book design copyright © 2008 by Tate Publishing, LLC. All rights reserved.
Cover & Interior design by Leah LeFlore

Published in the United States of America

ISBN: 978-1-60604-055-3
1. Sports and Recreation: Coaching: Basketball
2. Autobiography: Sports: Basketball
08.05.27

This book is dedicated to my wonderful wife, Joan, who passed away in 2007. She was a continual inspiration to me and a dedicated mother to our three sons, a dear friend to their wives, and loving grandmother to our grandchildren.

TABLE OF CONTENTS

INTRODUCTION

The following story is an overview of the true-life experiences of a basketball coach and an educator. The name of the coach is Cecil Mosenson whose career started in a fantasy-like world at Overbrook High School in Philadelphia, Pa. Cecil graduated from Temple University and felt coaching basketball and teaching were his calling. He was offered the coaching position at his old high school, Overbrook, at the ripe old age of twenty-two. Since he played at Overbrook on the basketball team, he was thrilled to return to a legendary basketball program that had a potentially great player. With this player and a strong supporting cast, Cecil quickly realized that his first year as a coach would be successful. Never did he believe that this player would become the player considered to be the greatest player to ever play the game of basketball. His name was Wilt Chamberlain. In addition, this first team would be thought of as the greatest high school basketball team in Pennsylvania. In fact, this team was considered one of the top 10 teams in high school history.

What a start to a career that would cover fifty years. Needless to say, these were great times, but with some difficulties, Cecil learned his profession well, got to understand all the complexities of his players. He began to fully appreciate the need to teach good habits, preaching fundamentals and the necessity for teamwork.

After a few years with this superstar and super teams, he had to make a decision about his future. He hoped to follow a path of marriage, children, and the need to provide for these responsibilities. His father needed him in the family business and the decision to help his family became a priority, although he clearly understood that what he achieved at Overbrook would never be relived and the glory days would just be fond memories. He remained with his father, but basketball and relationships with young athletes never left him. He would attend games and found himself coaching from the stands. His mind would wonder off, and he would think if he really could achieve again what he had with Wilt. Cecil was tormented with trying to make a choice of staying with the family business or returning to the hectic world of coaching basketball in a secondary school setting. He found that he terribly missed the thrill of coaching, the roar of the crowd, and the desire to make boys into men through excellent coaching and being the role model for all of them.

Cecil made the choice and accepted a teaching and coaching position in a suburban Philadelphia high school. With a return to coaching, Cecil set realistic goals—some were met and some were not. He was then coaching and teaching at Upper Moreland High School, which had a fine basketball tradition that was previously directed by a legendary coach who was now the principal. Cecil spent fifteen years in this position and generally reached his goals with an array of good teams and a few fair teams. Certainly, he had no Wilt Chamberlain. His teams played up to their potential, always looking well coached and disciplined. During one season, he tied for the BuxMont league championship, and a few other seasons his teams came in second. His tenure in this position was considered successful. The years at this school never rivaled his fabulous years at Overbrook, but he was pleased with the team's successes.

After his thirteenth year as coach at Upper Moreland, he became certified in administration and was appointed to an assistant principal's position. The following two years, Cecil moved to William Tennent in Warminster, Pa. where he took a similar position as assistant principal. After a short stint at that school, he was appointed to the principal's position at Tredyffrin Easttown Junior High School, a prestigious Upper Main Line School District in Berwyn, Pa. This stop in his illustrious career lasted fifteen years and carried him through difficult years, culminating in being honored by President Reagan in the Rose Garden of the White House. His school was selected as one of the outstanding junior high schools in the country. Cecil obviously felt that this award equaled his great success as a basketball coach in a very special different way. At this point, Cecil felt that he had done his best with achievements in basketball and school administration. He decided to retire and enjoy more time with his growing family and friends. He then wrote a book about his experiences as a principal entitled, *Mr. Principal, Your Activity Period Sucks!* It was a best seller in the Philadelphia area.

However, like all ex-coaches, after a time away from coaching, he got the desire to give basketball another try. Cecil applied and was accepted for a coaching position at William Tennent High School. This appointment, little did he know, would challenge him more than any other challenge that he faced in his many years of coaching. Tennent had no history of success in basketball, and other interests dominated the students' activities. Cecil felt ready for the challenge. He, a few years earlier, had been an assistant principal at this school district and was willing to accept this new responsibility. He was well aware of what that would require. The challenge was, he thought at that time, going to be exciting. Little did he know how exciting.

He gave it all he had, using every tool he learned as a coach in his previous positions. His early squads struggled. Knowing just the basics of the game, his team won few games during his first eight years.

Cecil and his players took the losses hard and no matter what he tried, the teams could not compete in this tough suburban league.

In his ninth season, he saw some light at the end of the tunnel. He had a few good players and after all the poundings, this squad ended with a 50/50 season. This was truly a great accomplishment for this school and the program. To Cecil, all the frustrations and hard work finally paid off.

In his final season, he had his best squad and their best season. He felt that he achieved his goal and brought basketball respectability to this fine school. An added reward was that his final team entered into the Pennsylvania Interscholastic Athletic Association playoffs and won, for the first time ever, in the first round against Conestoga, but then lost against a heavily favored opponent, Hatboro, in the next round. His final year at this school was one that rivaled his feelings of the Overbrook era in terms of satisfaction. He left this coaching position with his head held high and a feeling of a job well done.

He later coached a United States 14–16 year old boys' basketball team in the European Games in Scotland for the Maccabi and won the Gold Medal. He finally ended his career by coaching ninth-grade girls for six years in Archbishop Carroll Catholic High School.

I applaud a great teacher, coach, and administrator. He made many young people into fine adults who achieved wonderful successes in sports and in their lives.

—GIL SHOR
An ex-player, coach, and dear friend for many years.

PART I—THE EARLY YEARS

I grew up in West Philadelphia at 42nd and Leidy and learned to play basketball in the Leidy Elementary schoolyard. We sometimes shot at a peach basket nailed to a telephone pole. I tried out for the Overbrook J.V. basketball team in tenth grade in 1945. The coach, who was the football varsity coach, did not seem to know anything about basketball. The only way that players could make the team was to run the length of the court, back and forth for five minutes. If you made fifty lay-ups in those five minutes you made the team. After 8 tries, I finally shot the fiftieth lay-up as he blew the whistle, signaling that time had expired. I made the team although I thought I was going to die from exhaustion. I played two minutes the entire season of a twenty-game schedule and that was when the varsity coach took over twice, getting me into each game one minute at a time. The following year I didn't make the varsity team during tryouts, but the coach let me practice with the team as a scrub, filling in whenever I was needed. In those days, students graduated in January and a few players left the team, so some openings were created. The first game of the new semester was to be played at Convention Hall in center city of Philadelphia. As if a miracle happened, I was put into the varsity's starting lineup. It's bad enough to start your career on your home court, but this was a major arena that seated thousands of fans. I didn't sleep for three days prior to the game. And the night of the game, I was shaking all over. We won and my debut was a success. I had ten points and no turnovers. I will never understand the logic behind this coach's thinking; however, I was now beginning to believe that I could improve my skills of the game through hard work, daily workouts, and just normal motivation. Each day when I took a bus and a trolley to get home, I would eat a quick dinner, and then get over to Haddington Recreation center in West Philadelphia, where fifty high school and college players would be playing into the wee hours of the night. I also was getting a feeling that I was beginning to understand the strategies of the game. At the same time, I started to sense that my future would be in the profession of teaching and coaching. I worked hard on my basketball skills all summer at an overnight camp. The next year in 1947, I was the starting shooting forward on our varsity, which was comprised of twelve Jewish players who won twenty straight games throughout the season. The team lost in the city championship to Bartram High School, which was coached by the legendary Menchy Goldblatt.

Our team was undefeated up until the Public League championship game, and we were playing Bartram High School for the title. We had already beaten them during the regular season. The game was played before a sellout crowd at the Penn Palestra in Philadelphia. Bartram's speed equalized our talent, and the game was tied going into the final seconds. In quick order, Bartram made two field goals, and the key goal was by Gil Shor (who wrote the introduction to this book). They won the game 42–37, the same point spread that we had beaten them by during the season. We were emotionally crushed. I remember looking up into the stands and seeing all of our fans crying. Our players just stood in the center of the court unable to move to the sideline. When I arrived home, I trembled as I opened the door feeling the effects of the loss while all the time knowing that my mother and father were always supportive of me. I was just so ashamed because we lost. I learned a great deal in that shocking loss. Basketball styles were changing. The game of passing-cutting off the pivot man and weaving the ball was being replaced with speed and the fast break. Pressing teams became more accepted by coaches. The two-handed set shot, which was my best shot, became obsolete and the jump shot became the method of operation. The early star jump shooter in the pros was Joe Fulks and every young athlete started to emulate him.

I was now laying the foundation for my future in coaching if the opportunity ever came.

Our entire starting five at Overbrook got scholarships to college. The players were Barry Love, who went to Lafayette, Larry Goldsborough who went to Cornell, Alan Stein who went to Columbia, and Stanley Gordon who went to Temple with me.

I was offered a scholarship to Temple and went on to play there. The Hall of Fame coach, Harry Litwack, was the freshman coach at that time and he loved my style of play. However, the varsity coach whose name was Josh Cody was a football coach and barely knew what a basketball looked like. Bill Mlkvy was the star of the team at that time and was a wonderful All-American player. The coach demanded that we should continuously pass the ball to Bill. I once scored eight points in the first minute of play, making all of my shots, and was pulled out of the game. I didn't play for the rest of the game because, in his narrow mind, I was shooting too much, but that could be the story for another book. In my senior year, I couldn't take the abuse from this coach and went on to play for a while with the Washington Generals team who always played against the Harlem Globetrotters. I was assigned by Reds Klotz, the perennial coach, to guard Marques Haynes, their wonderful dribbler, who always was allowed to make fools of our players. I then played in the Eastern Professional League in Harrisburg, Pa. for 4 years with Norm Grekin, a LaSalle College star. Our team was coached by the legendary

**The 1947-48 Overbrook High School
Basketball Team**
*Back Row—Mel Kates, Stan Gordon, Al Kates
Front Row—Cecil Mosenson, Alan Stein, Barry Love, Larry
Golsborough*

Philadelphia Spha's (South Philadelphia Hebrew Association) player, Cy Kasselman.

After graduation from Overbrook, I majored in physical education at Temple, and when I was a senior, I was lucky enough to be assigned to teach as a student teacher at Overbrook. It was there that Sam Cozen, who taught physical education and who was also the school's current basketball coach, took a liking to me. He was ending his high-school coaching career and was moving on to coach Drexel University. That opened up the basketball position. I applied, never dreaming that I would even be considered. Here was an inner-city, twenty-two-year-old kid with no experience applying for a basketball job at a premier basketball school, Overbrook High School, and was inheriting Wilt Chamberlain, who was going to be a national basketball phenomenon. I knew Wilt since I had played previously against him in some independent games. The summer passed and there was not a word about the appointment and suddenly, out of nowhere, I got a call from the athletic director, Ben Ogden. He asked me if I was still interested in the job. How can I explain my emotions? My heart started racing and I began to shake and stutter on the phone. The only caveat was that I would have to teach English part time and physical education part time. I was a decent student, but to teach an English course in a high school gave me quivers. I would have to become temporarily certified by taking many English courses. These were two challenges that would make any grown man become unnerved to say the least. Of course, I said, "yes sir," but I didn't get any sleep for the next three years. I accepted the position and began teaching in the fall of 1953.

Cecil Mosenson - 1950

PART II—COACHING
WILT CHAMBERLAIN

The clock showed 1:50 remaining in the last quarter. We were down four points to the McKeesport Tigers in the Farrell Invitational Tournament at Johnstown. We had just played Farrell the night before and lost at the buzzer. Farrell and McKeesport were recognized as the two best teams in the state and we were invited to play them in this special tournament.

I called my Overbrook team around me and told them to feed the ball to Wilt. But Chamberlain was being guarded like a convict in Alcatraz; two Tiger players were with him constantly. During the last 1:10 seconds of the game with the jammed field house in a complete uproar, the teams scored a total of nineteen points, and somehow Wilt broke loose to score ten of them. We took the lead with twenty seconds left and went on to win 75–74. He scored forty-six points and played with courage when we needed him. I have always thought of that game as the high point of Wilt's career. His tremendous competitive spirit and greatness under pressure came of age that night. It was a pleasure to be his coach—most of the time.

Months earlier on my first night as a coach, I was nervous as a cat. I had Wilt, but having him was part of my concern. He was starting his second season at Overbrook High School (he was a junior) and was already a schoolboy phenomenon. I was just a rookie coach. I remember saying to myself, "Everybody expects me to win because I acquired the big guy, but what happens if I lose?" Our opponent was South Catholic coached by Jack Kraft—no pushover under any circumstances. The first two quarters were close and, at that point, we led by only 3 points. But I needn't have worried. My team broke the game open in the second half and we won easily. Wilt scored forty-five points and continuously batted away South Catholic's attempts at the basket.

People have always asked me what kind of person was Wilt. My answer is always the same. *He had real character.* There was a lot of delinquency around Overbrook at that time, but he always was above it. He came from a really good home life and it showed. He was a good student also. Most of his grades were B's and what he got, he earned. As a junior, Wilt was shy. He was painfully conscious of his height and long spindly shanks. We were told that the large scars on the fronts of his legs came from working in the cotton fields in the South as a youngster. He wore high socks to cover the scars and used rubber bands for garters. This is why he always wore a rubber band on his wrist in games; he used it as a spare. On occasion, he was a prankster. One day when a group of us were in the Overbrook coaches' office, we got to kidding Wilt about how strong he was. Suddenly, he picked up big Ed Veith, the football coach who weighed about 220 pounds, put him on his hip like a twenty-pound sack of potatoes, and walked off down the hallway. But other times Wilt, as a junior, became moody and sullen for periods at a time. He would retreat into a shell that was almost impossible to penetrate.

Wilt was destined for stardom. He was 6'11" tall with a wing span of 7'2." His hands from wrist to fingertip measured 9 1/2 inches. He held a basketball as though it were a grapefruit. In his junior year, he had a strong dislike for authority. Not long into that first season, we had our first major run-in. It happened during the Frankford game. During the warm-ups, I was talking to the other coach and the officials when I happened to glance at Wilt. He had adorned himself with a golf cap, a shimmering white silk scarf, and dark sunglasses. He looked like something out of *Mad Magazine.* I called him over and told him very directly to get rid of those glad rags.

We went into our pre-game huddle, but he kept looking the other way and apparently not listening to me. The game was three minutes old when I realized what was happening. Wilt was angry and was refusing to shoot. He would pass every time to a teammate. I called timeout and discussed the matter. I got no response, so I pulled him out of the game. My face was white with anger. I gave him a few choice words at the half, but only got a sullen stare. I put him into the game again midway into the third quarter and I yanked him out again. This went on until the last few minutes of the game. I put him in once more, he scored, and we won the game although it was close. To say that I was exasperated and angry was putting it mildly. I had a private session with him after the game, and I thought we definitely had an understanding about what I expected. He was not going to try that stunt again. I was not going to give him a second chance. It worked for the next game because he scored seventy-one points. But even seventy-one points didn't really represent his potential. He had big, steady hands, excellent reflexes, wide-angle vision, great strength, marvelous agility, and, of course, all that height and reach. He even had a good feel for dribbling; a rare thing for tall players in those days. Moreover, he had more stamina than any athlete I had known. Some of his feats were almost unbelievable.

Sometimes on a shot by an opposing player, Wilt would leap, grab the ball with one hand, trapping it against the backboard, and in the same instant before coming down would fling it out to the breaking guard. He then would sprint down the court, take a high pass, and dunk the ball through the net. Often, at such times, the opposing players would just shake their heads and give up.

The dunk shot was scarcely known until Wilt came along. With his ability to go two and a half feet higher than the rim, and with his great strength, he could ram the ball down into the net with such force that sometimes he ripped the net. Since there was no goaltending rule, Wilt could roam the lane and swat the ball as it approached the basket. The crowds went wild.

The next year, Wilt scored seventy-four points early in the season against Roxborough, and we all knew that we were going to play that same team a second time. The game was going to be in the Overbrook gym, which only seated 300 people. The Friday before the game, the practice was lousy since everyone was whooping it up for a new Chamberlain record. I called the team together and told them we were not going to humiliate the other team. The team responded; however, Wilt was going to test me again. He fairly blazed with unspoken defiance. His belligerence was so obvious that it had to be addressed. I whirled on him and said, "If you don't like the way I'm running the team, get out of the gym and don't come back." I was fed up, I had enough of his rebellious mannerisms. He got up and left the gym. I started practice again, using plays that did not include his presence. The rest of the team looked stunned.

I went to the principal and said, "You better prepare a press release. I just threw Chamberlain off the team." His face became ashen and I thought that he was going to faint.

His response was, "Let's wait until Monday and maybe something positive will happen."

It was a long weekend. I realized that I had just kicked the greatest high school player in the country off the team.

On Monday, I saw Wilt several times in the hallways and he looked the other way. He walked straight past me. At practice time, I walked into the gym and there was the big guy shooting baskets.

His face was completely expressionless. As I stood looking at him, not knowing what to expect, he approached me with a ball in his hands. I could not imagine what was coming next. He put the ball into my hands and sort of looked at me with his head down. He paused for a long time, and then asked me if I would help him with his hook shot.

The crisis was over. However, I needed to go to my athletic director and tell him that when we played this team again there was a possibility for a national record, at the expense of this other team. I was uncomfortable about that prospect, but I needed to be fair to Wilt. His advice was that records are broken all of the time and since he, the athletic director, was also a track coach, his analogy was that he doesn't tell his sprinters to slow down when they are winning.

The next evening, just before we took the floor against Roxborough, I told the boys that we would play our normal game with a tight defense and take our shots when we could. Obviously fearful of Wilt and the possibility of a record being broken, the

Roxborough team started the game by not shooting and trying to stall and waste time on the clock. They seldom tried to work the ball down the court. They just tried to retain possession of the ball and hardly ever attempted shots. By half time I was thoroughly annoyed with their stalling tactics. I figured if they were determined to slow the game down, we were justified in speeding it up. At half time, Wilt had twenty-six points and it was clear to me that our relationship was where I had hoped it would be. I leaned over to him and told him that if he could break the record, he had my blessing. When I took him out with 2 1/2 minutes remaining in the game, he had ninety points. He had scored sixty-four points in 13 1/2 minutes. At one point, he scored fifteen points in one minute.

He thanked me after the game for allowing him to break the record.

Other coaches knocked themselves out planning defenses against our team. In most cases, their plans included putting two to four tall men in to guard Wilt. Coach Al Webb of Germantown High even put all five men on Wilt. I simply moved the big guy to the corner of the court and the five defenders followed him. The rest of my team had a real party, passing and shooting at leisure.

THE VILLANOVA SCRIMMAGE

As I mentioned, we were invited to play two games during the Christmas break against the best teams in the state, Farrell and McKeesport, on consecutive nights. A week before we were to leave, I became concerned that we had not yet played against stiff competition, so I asked Al Severance, the coach of Villanova, if it would be possible to scrimmage his team on their court. It was a shot in the dark. Usually college teams would not dare to scrimmage high school teams for fear of being embarrassed. However, they were getting ready to play Dayton and that team had a player who was seven-foot tall. Severance thought that Wilt and the rest of our team would be good experience for his players to compete against. We scrimmaged them only once, although the players still have different opinions whether we scrimmaged them once or twice and who really won the scrimmage(s).

The scrimmage lasted for about three hours and no total score was kept. After each quarter, the points were taken off the scoreboard and the clock started over again. Our managers, however, kept a running score and the final tally favored our team by a large margin. In all fairness, I seem to remember their star, Bob Schaeffer, did not play. Bob Powers, then a sophomore guard was quoted in the Daily News, "In a strange way, we were honored. We knew what quality was. We knew that greatness was going to come Wilt's way. There wasn't any flicker of any of us being upset." He goes on to say, "We had a practice on a Friday night and Mr. Severance got us together afterward." He said, "He wanted us to know we were having a scrimmage at 8 o'clock the next morning, but he wouldn't tell us who we were playing." We went to the field house the next morning. One door was open. This is a building with about twenty doors. Just one was open. All of a sudden we saw big Wilt and his teammates arrive. We were all looking at each other. 'What's going on?'

"We scrimmaged for about three hours with no spectators. We usually played a five-man weave. That was our offense. We laughed about it afterwards. There was no chance Wilt was coming out to Nova to play against a five-man weave." Powers went on to say that he greatly admired Wilt and his teammates. "The big guy was very congenial, very polite. He was a very nice man as were all of his friends." Powers continued, "Wilt was such a hero to so many people. He had just as many friends that were not of his race as there were of his race. Kids in the ghetto, kids in the suburbs should all know about Wilt. What a life's story."

THE FARRELL GAME

The athletic director, Ben Ogden, had approved an air flight to Farrell. I didn't recall at the time a high school team ever flying to any part of the state to play a game. The tournament directors had agreed to allow us to be waived into the finals of each game instead of requiring us to play in the semifinals. We were incredibly excited. This was going to be our first flight anywhere. None of the members on the team, including me, had ever flown before. Most of us arrived at the airport in plenty of time. The parents arranged to bring the players to the airport. I started a head count to see if everyone was there and much to my surprise, one player was missing. He was my starting shooting forward, Jimmy Sadler. We waited, and waited. We called his home and there was no answer. I asked the attendant in charge of the flight if the plane could be delayed for a while. With much hesitation after checking with the powers to be, he agreed to hold the departure for fifteen minutes. You can't believe how quickly fifteen minutes can pass when you are having a nervous breakdown. The attendant came to me and said that we must board the aircraft now and that we had to move very quickly. I directed the players to board the plane and I was going to be the last one on. As I was stepping through the doorway, I took one last look and I thought I saw someone running toward the plane. It was Jimmy. He had a suitcase under one arm and his basketball handbag in the other hand. He waved to me and ran up the runway onto the plane. I didn't have time to ask him why he was late, but I made sure that he sat next to me on the plane. I loved this guy and he never did anything that caused me angina. He looked at me sheepishly and I did not want to ask him at this time what had happened. I knew that he would tell me. He started out by apologizing and said in a very quiet tone that he had just gotten married an hour ago. He quickly kissed his wife goodbye, ran and got a taxi, and got here as fast as he could. I did not ask him any questions.

We finally were on our way. We flew out to Farrell and prepared to play these important games on Friday and Saturday.

The emotions were high not only for the players but for the entire two cities. This may have been a once in a lifetime tournament for the fans.

This was our first time away from the Philadelphia area and the first time we faced a screaming, emotionally soaked, hostile crowd. The Steelers were razor sharp that night. Their all-court press was working and they had a physically tight man-to-man defense. Wilt was fouled almost every time he received the ball. This was the other team's strategy. With seconds to go, Farrell was ahead 59–58 and we had the ball out of bounds, under our basket. Our key play in such a situation was for Jimmy Sadler to fling the ball sky high to Wilt. The ball was thrown in and Wilt was pushed into the stands. No whistle and the time ran out. If the officials had blown their whistles, they would have been hanged from the rafters right there. We lost that game. I did receive a large number of letters from the fans in the stands telling us that Farrell did not deserve to win.

There was one game against West Philly that remains with me all these years. West Philly coached by Doug Connelly always had a great team and the rivalry was always intense. In fact West Philly only lost 6 games in 3 years during that era (two each year to Overbrook). In Wilt's final year, the game was played at Sayre Junior High School because that court could accommodate the very large crowds for the rivalry. West Philly had an outstanding guard by the name of Joey Goldenberg who later became that school's all-time winning coach, and another player by the name of Chink Scott who was their center at 6'9" tall. Sometime near the end of the first half, some tempers got a little heated between two players and the rest of the players started to get involved. All of a sudden, Wilt raised his two hands in the middle of the court as he saw many of the people in the stands starting to come down onto the playing floor. As if by magic, all the fans stopped in their tracks, turned around, and started to move back into the stands. It looked to me as if he were holding the Ten Commandments in one hand and his other hand was pointing upward into the heavens. He was Charlton Heston of the basketball world. The game finished without further incident. I never saw Wilt raise a fist or ever get angry at any player during his basketball career no matter how physical they were to him.

I would not be realistic if I tried to take credit for Wilt's greatness. He would have become a star with any coach or without a coach at all. Some help was required, however, with his dribbling, passing, and offensive positioning. He responded well to this coaching. What I couldn't get him to do was develop a variety of shots instead of just depending on his dunk shot and that terrible fade away jumper. I pushed him on these things, trying to get him to shoot hook shots moving toward the basket. At that time, he didn't need those moves; he was taking the league apart as it was. I tried to stress that sometime down the road he was going to need additional moves. I did have some fun with him, playing "horse" or shooting long shots with him and even sometimes letting him win. Maybe I should have acted more like a drill sergeant, and drilled him on these moves until he mastered them. But Wilt was complicated with his shifting moods. He was facing social pressures generated by his conspicuous height, his early fame, his life amidst the racial tensions of a big city, and his adolescence. Only by degrees did he respond to my friendship and authority. It was reasonable to think that tough, rigid drilling at this stage might have made him a better player, but it wouldn't have made him a better person. I really did like Wilt and the biggest thing I did for him was to become his friend.

Wilt's final spring was hectic. It seemed as if every college coach in the country was after him. He was offered 120 scholarships. They plowed him under with a blizzard of offers. They phoned us constantly, and their recruiters camped—almost literally—on our doorsteps. For the most part, I enjoyed the recruiting period and Wilt enjoyed his fame, but was irritated by the recruiters. They came with loads of adulation, and since he thought they were out to exploit him, he despised them. Sometimes he was indifferent to them, sometimes blunt, and sometimes even hostile.

Wilt and I became a traveling team. Wilt went to Michigan and Michigan State. He and I then visited Indiana University and the University of Detroit. After those trips, the Philadelphia philanthropist, Fredric Mann of the Mann Music Center, took us in his personal chauffeured car to visit the famous Harry Winston's Jeweler, one of the world's largest and most prestigious jewelry empires on 5th Ave. in New York. He offered Wilt any choice of jewelry he wanted if he would attend the University of Pennsylvania. Offers came from the Ivy League, Big Ten, Big Seven, Missouri Valley, Pacific Coast Conference, and the leading independents. In almost every case, he was told something like this, "Enroll in our school and we will beat any offer." One alumnus promised a much higher-paid job for his father. His father, at the time, was a custodian in a factory. Another alumnus was willing to sponsor Wilt through undergraduate school and law school. Wilt was offered room, board, campus jobs, and money, which was to be paid in monthly installments by wealthy alumni. A big school in Southern California even guaranteed him a job in a Hollywood studio. A Southern university wrote to him and said, "You will be the first Negro ever to enter our university," and Wilt wrote back, "The next will be your first. I'm not interested." Phog Allen of Kansas was the winner in the great Chamberlain sweepstakes. He made a campaign of it. No Madison Avenue promotion was ever prepared with greater care. He even enlisted African American leaders from Kansas to get in touch with Wilt and assigned Kansas teachers to contact him.

Phog Allen, himself, was the big man of the campaign. He opened it by flying to Philadelphia on the evening we played Germantown High. From the airport he went directly to Wilt's home and enlisted Wilt's mother. Phog once declared, "I always head for the mother, you know, I'm a momma's guy." Indeed, he was a charmer. Phog addressed Wilt's mother and, in his most charming manner said to her, "Mrs. Chamberlain, now I know why Wilt is such a nice, young man."

Then, Phog went to the Germantown court. I didn't know that he was around until he came up to me at the end of the game. After we chatted a bit, I told him that I didn't know if Wilt was interested in Kansas or if he would even sit down to talk about it. Just then, Wilt came out of the dressing room and Phog rushed over and introduced himself. Wilt apparently didn't catch the name or maybe didn't know who Phog Allen was. He looked at me with a dumbfounded expression and asked, "Who is this guy?"

"It's Phog Allen, the coach of Kansas, and he wants us to visit Kansas."

Wilt turned to Allen and said, "I'm not interested in going to Kansas. Don't waste your time." With that, Wilt spun around and walked away.

Phog wasn't deterred in the least. He simply invited himself along to a nearby banquet where Wilt was to receive the Cliveden award as Philadelphia's outstanding African American athlete. We walked three abreast down the sidewalk with Phog talking a mile a minute. When we got to the banquet, Allen introduced himself to the master of ceremonies and was invited to sit with Wilt and me at the speaker's table. He sat down between us. Later he was called on to make a speech and responded with an oration about Kansas, motherhood, basketball, integrity, and Wilt. He then looked right at Wilt's mother and said, "If I were to pick a school for Wilt, I'd pick one where he would be safe." Mrs. Chamberlain beamed. Both before and after the speech, Phog spouted an endless stream of humor and sports' stories. Toward the end of the evening, Wilt began to warm to him. After the banquet, Phog gave us a final invitation to visit Kansas and left for the airport.

Several days later, I persuaded Wilt that we

should go out and look the Kansas situation over. I liked Phog Allen and I knew that the coaching staff was top drawer and so was the basketball program. Our plane left very late from Philadelphia on a bitterly cold, wintery evening. At 3:30 in the morning, we landed in Kansas City, and we were met by a twelve-man delegation that included some senators, businessmen, some African American leaders, some journalists, and two of Phog's sons. They greeted us as if we were the only people left in the world. After a few hours sleep at a booster's home in Lawrence, Kansas, we sat down to a Kansas steak breakfast with scrambled eggs and luscious pastries. Afterward Phog took us on a tour of the campus. That evening Wilt was met by a group of students and was taken to a fraternity house. My back was hurting me, so Phog Allen, who was also an amateur chiropractor, took me into his den and proceeded to give me a treatment. As he was giving me the treatment, he was also selling me on the idea that Wilt must come to Kansas. A private meeting was also set up with the boosters to further encourage me to get Wilt to enroll in the university. Wilt did not make any decisions at that time and a second trip was set up. My wife and I were also invited to accompany Wilt.

THE KANSAS DECISION

Phog Allen told Wilt that the new field house that had a 17,000-seat capacity was being built for him to accommodate the crowds that would be coming to see him play. As to what else Kansas offered Wilt, Phog replied, "I will do whatever it takes to get him to enroll at Kansas." However, Phog was never in on the direct clandestine negotiations with selective Kansas boosters concerning Wilt's decision to go to Kansas. Phog Allen did offer me a job to be his assistant. In fact, my wife and I bought a new Buick to drive to Kansas.

However, several months later Phog had to resign his coaching position since he became seventy years old and the law prohibited him from continuing, although he thought the authorities would overlook that provision because of his public popularity as a basketball coach. Our agreement was voided, probably much to the relief of my wife and me, since we had many intense discussions and much apprehension concerning this dramatic move from the Philadelphia area that we loved. Dick Harp then became the coach. There was a great deal of interest throughout the newspaper world and the NCAA concerning the reasons for Wilt's selection to Kansas. In fact, I was invited to attend an Army/Navy game that year at Franklin Field by a famous New York newspaperman who offered me substantial financial inducements to disclose the reason for

Wilt's acceptance to this Mid-Western school. I was not in a position to satisfy his request. On the way home from the second visit, while flying between Kansas City and Chicago, Wilt, with discussions with me, made his decision to go to Kansas. The incentives were far too great to turn down.

Wilt's last game with me was against West Catholic for the City championship. It was played in the Palestra. The previous day's practice, I could see that the players were somewhat nervous especially my 6'5 shooting forward Vince Miller. He usually shot a jump shot with great accuracy from the corner when Wilt was double-teamed.

During this practice, he could not make a shot and I could see that he was becoming frustrated. The practice ended and I told him that he and I were going to stay in the gym all night if we had to, so that he could get his rhythm back and his comfort level to where it should be. At about 8 pm after over 200 hundred shots from the corner with no one in the gym but just him and me, I decided he had enough. He was exhausted, but I felt that he was back on track. I didn't know if I had done the right thing by wearing him out or if I should have just let him rest. He scored 31 points and had his best game ever in the Palestra that had thousands of screaming fans. Wilt ended up with 35 points and Jimmy Sadler, our young married friend, had 17 points.

Ironically, Wilt was almost locked out of this final high school game. I was sitting near the court before the game when a manager ran over to me and told me excitedly that they wouldn't let Wilt in. I quickly went to the gate and sure enough, there was the big fellow on the outside. He didn't have his ticket; all players, as well as fans, needed a ticket to get into the game. The ticket takers were adamant. "Our instructions are to let no one into the game without a ticket and this guy doesn't have one and we don't care who he is." I went back to find our athletic director, who also happened to be the commissioner of the Public and Catholic leagues, and told him my story. He finally convinced the ticket takers to allow Wilt to enter. Mr. Ogden gave him a good rebuke and sent him to the dressing room. We won easily, 83–42. I later learned that Wilt had sold his ticket.

My relationship with the members of the team was great.

We all got along well. Ira Davis, the captain, was the real leader of the team and was highly respected by everyone. He also was a track star at Overbrook and at college, and later he represented the United States in the Olympics and continued his career as the track coach at LaSalle University.

Many times during the season and after the season, my wife and I would have the team over for dinner. I always remember that Wilt had to lower his head when walking into the dining room. He could eat three veal cutlets at a time and drink a whole large bottle of soda. We never knew how much to buy when the guys came over. There were times when the boys would cut my bushes outside of my house; my excited neighbors would come over to get autographs and just watch them.

There have been many basketball rules that were changed because of Wilt's phenomenal abilities.

Goaltending was the first of many rules that was changed because of Wilt. Another rule that was established was the widening of the foul lane from 6 feet to 12 feet to eliminate Wilt's advantage of putting the ball back into the basket on a missed shot. A third rule established an invisible barrier on the foul line which stopped Wilt from quickly following up missed foul shots and dunking the ball.

Wilt's accomplishments are legendary. He went on to play at Kansas for three years. In his fourth year he signed a lucrative deal with Abe Saperstein to play for the Harlem Globetrotters. That following year, he signed to play with the Philadelphia Warriors, owned by Eddie Gottlieb at that time. Eddie gave me a lifetime pass to the NBA, but sold the team a few years later. And that lifetime pass agreement was never conveyed to the new owners.

THE COLLEGE DILEMMA

I have been asked at least a thousand times over these past fifty years, "What was the deal that sent Wilt to Kansas?"

Let me present a point of view shared by many for sports' fans to think about.

When Wilt graduated from high school in 1955, the NBA in an unprecedented move allowed him to be drafted by the Philadelphia Warriors in 1959, since he was considered to be a territorial draft pick. The NBA made this exception to its rule solely for Chamberlain. It stated that when Wilt's college class graduated, he could play with the Philadelphia Warriors owned by Eddie Gottlieb. Mr. Gottlieb, at that time, was a powerful executive for the professional league and wielded much influence. The professional contract signed by Wilt with the Warriors was $100,000. The year before, after three years at Kansas, Wilt signed a contract with the Harlem Globetrotters for $50,000.

The National Collegiate Athletic Association, which governs college athletics, stated that athletes could receive tuition, room, and board in college, which Wilt obviously was to receive. Money was never to be exchanged or the athlete would be ineligible to play.

Wilt was told previously in conversations with Phog Allen, the Kansas coach, that the university was building a 17,000-seat capacity field house and that Wilt was going to fill it every game, if he enrolled at Kansas.

This is the issue.

Assuming that for the four years that Wilt was going to attend Kansas, he would play approximately fifty home games filling the field house each time. The income from these games would be astronomical for the university. As an example of his drawing power, Wilt scored 50 points as a freshman against the varsity in a pre-season game that rarely had any attendance. The field house at this game had 15,000 people. Was he entitled to more than an athletic scholarship? Were the current restrictions too great? Should there have been some kind of exception for this super star or other super stars? Were these athletes being taken advantage of by the guidelines of the college governing bodies, or the 1959 standards of the National Basketball Association.

The rules by the NBA have been changed many times as the rule makers continue to struggle to find an answer that will satisfy everyone. Many other sporting teams allow college students to participate with professional teams. The new 2007 rule recently instituted by the NBA mandates that high school athletes must stay in college for one year before turning pro. This policy has the potential to decimate the basketball teams of those colleges that have recruited those high-power athletes. In the seventies, the professional rules allowed players such as Moses Malone to play in the pros directly out of high school.

As a direct result of the NBA rules, Wilt could not play in the NBA during his college years. This policy continuously irked him and it was the deciding factor why Wilt left Kansas to play for the Harlem Globetrotters.

His personal situation didn't require a college education for his future. Was he therefore entitled to financial benefits as a result of his drawing power? He certainly did not need to go to college to get a degree. His financial future was secure by his basketball athleticism.

Over the years, there has been much discussion about the value of superior athletes and whether they should be paid for their services at the college level. I realize that the discussion is highly controversial, but in this particular situation, Wilt was used strictly as a financial reservoir for Kansas University throughout his college career.

In his professional career, Wilt won two NBA championships and was inducted into the Naismith Memorial Basketball Hall Of Fame.

WILT CHAMBERLAIN'S CAREER ACHIEVEMENTS

- Scored 100 points against Knicks, Hershey Pa.
- Most 40-point in a season, 63 times (1961–62)
- Most career regular season 40-point games: 271
- Most consecutive 50-point games: 7 times (December 16, 1961-December 29, 1961)
- Most career 60-point games: 32 times
- Most consecutive season leading league in points: 7
- Most points per game by a rookie NBA player: 37.6 (1959–60)
- Most points by a rookie in a single season: 2,707 (1959–60)
- Most free throws made in a game: 28 against Knicks (1962)
- Scored 50 points as a rookie against Boston Celtics (1960)
- Most consecutive field goals without a miss in the game: 18/18 (1967)
- 33 straight wins with the Los Angeles Lakers.
- 4,029 points and 2,052 rebounds in one season (1961–62)
- 55 rebounds in one game.
- 50.4 points per game (1961–62)
- Career field goal average: 72.7%
- Career rebounds: 23,924
- Led NBA in scoring 7 years in a row.
- In 118 games, he scored 50 points or more.

- Led NBA in assists (1967–68)
- *But for all of his accomplishments, Overbrook was the place where he wanted to be remembered the most.*

KUTSHERS IN THE CATSKILLS

In the late fifties, I spent some wonderful summers at Kutsher's Country Club in Monticello, New York, which is in the Catskill Mountains. I was the assistant athletic director and Kutshers had hired some novice basketball coach by the name of Red Auerbach to be the director of the poker games at this resort. His additional responsibility was to treat all the New York women with dignity and care. A side responsibility was to coach some of the waiters and busboys who thought that they could play basketball. I was to assist him by sitting quietly on the bench next to him. I remember some of the names of the players because their heads and shoulders were well over everyone else's heads. They were not very good at carrying trays, but, boy could they play basketball.

In the late fifties, all of the country clubs had the best players in the country competing against each other. Some of the country clubs were Grossinger, Concord, and Nevele. The league was called the Borsch Belt. Our team was comprised of the following players: Frank Ramsey, who later became the outstanding sixth man on the championship Boston Celtics, Cliff Hagan, also played for the Celtics until he and Ed Macauley were traded to St. Louis for some kid by the name of Bill Russell. Sihigo Green played for Duquesne and the Rochester Royals, Togo Palazzi was Holy Cross's greatest player, Rip Gish was an outstanding player for Western Kentucky, and Bobby Watson starred at Kentucky. Milton and Helen Kutsher were the owners and there was not a nicer couple than these two. The only thing that bothered me was that when we won a game, which was every time, Red would light up a cigar and always offered me a cigar. When he finally realized that I wouldn't smoke one of his cigars, he insisted that I take a puff and I always choked on it. We spent a few wonderful summers together and a few years later, Wilt worked at Kutshers as a bellhop. He could carry four suitcases at a time and the patrons just loved him. My grandson, Jeffrey, years later, was in charge of organizing the fans so that they could get autographs from the players and especially the big guy.

Each year, Wilt attended the Maurice Stokes Memorial game, first as a player and then as a famous spectator. The Maurice Stokes Memorial game was organized by Jack Twyman, an NBA player of the former Rochester Royals. He became the legal guardian of Maurice Stokes, who was paralyzed due to the after effects of a head injury suffered during the final game of 1958 regular season. The game at Kutsher's Country Club raised money for medical expenses for Maurice Stokes. 1998 was Wilt's last year there. Wilt died October 14, the next year.

In the picture below is Jeffrey and Joanna Mosenson with Wilt at Kutsher's Country Club. (1998)

- Ira Davis: U.S. Olympic participant in the hop-step-jump event in 1956. Track and field coach at LaSalle College.
- Vinson Miller: Successful high school basketball coach at Frankford High School.
- Doug Leaman: Successful basketball coach at Adelphia College and Lower Moreland High School.
- Melvin Brodsky: Temple University basketball player, principal in the Upper Darby School District.
- Jimmy Sadler: Sales manager at Seagrams for 36 years.
- Allan Weinberg: Senior vice president at Wachovia.
- Marty Hughes: Computer Analyst at M.I.T.
- Marvin Kravitz: Notable dentist.
- Reds Guralnick: Successful salesman.
- Irv Jaffe: Acountant.
- Dave Shapiro: Successful businessman.

1953-54

Coach Mosenson, Doug Leaman, Allan Weinberg, Marvin Kravitz, Ira Davis, Edward Boykin, Reds Guralnick, Melvin Brodsky, Jimmy Sadler, Lou Sadler, Dave Henryhand, Wilt Chamberlain

1954–55

Allan Weinberg, Irv Jaffe, Dave Shapiro, Wilt, Vinson Miller, Jimmy Sadler, Biddy Johnson, Coach Mosenson
Ted Wexler, Doug Leaman, Marty Hughes, Tom Fitzhugh, Jordan Goldman

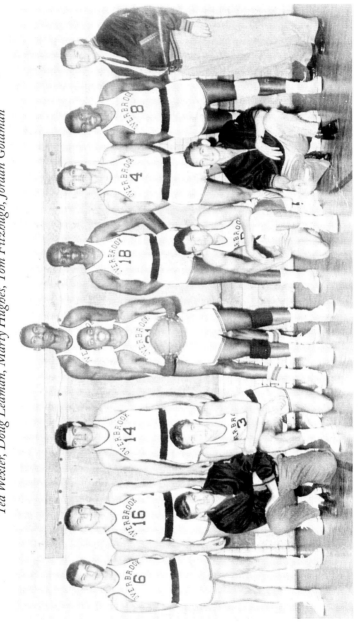

Coach Mosenson and Wilt

Wilt and Jimmy Sadler

Wilt Dunking Ball (Overbrook gym)

Wilt with MVP plaque

Wilt palming two basketballs

**Markward club award
1953–54**

Working out at Kutsher's Countryclub

**Allan Weinberg (14) Wilt
Dave Shapiro (10) Irv Jaffe (8)**

Wilt as a freshman at Kansas

REFLECTIONS

Doug Leaman 1952–1954 *Overbrook*

I want you to know that I have always admired you. Those who played with you and those who watched you, rank you up there with the best. Your ability as a basketball player and coach far exceeded normal expectations. When Phog Allen came to see Wilt at the Germantown game, I had one of my best shooting nights. I think I made 5 out of 6 long shots. The 3-point shot was not a part of the game at that time. I didn't know that the Kansas coach was in the stands. Although he was there to see Wilt, a light must have gone on in his brain, probably thinking that if I went to Kansas maybe that would somehow entice Wilt to go there too. He offered me a scholarship to Kansas a short time later. In fact, Wilt and I drove to Kansas together in Wilt's Oldsmobile. Wilt drove most of the way because I always started to fall asleep driving. When we got near the border of Kansas, we stopped for a hamburger at one of the food places and the guy would not serve Wilt. He wanted him to eat in the back of the kitchen somewhere. I think Wilt was ready to turn back and go home, but I convinced him to keep going. However, we drove quickly away without eating and arrived at Phog Allen's house very late at night. He and his family were all asleep. We woke them up and, I think, we slept on his sofa and on the floor that night and went to the dorms the next day. I only stayed at Kansas one week. I was home sick and had a girlfriend in Philadelphia and I needed to get back home. I later enrolled at Saint Joseph's College and played a short time under Jack Ramsey. He was using a pressing defense and I just did not have the physical ability to play that kind of defense.

It's funny what you remember from the Overbrook years. On our very small court, the stands surrounded the out of bounds lines, so that when I took the ball out to throw it in, the girls sitting in the front row would tickle my legs and pinch my rump. I sometimes lost my composure and found it hard to concentrate especially if the girls were cute.

The courts were so small in those days that at South Catholic, when I shot my two-handed set shot, it would always hit the ceiling so that I had to alter the arc of my shot, which ruined my percentages. Saint Thomas More had pillars in the side of the court so I had to dribble around them to pass the ball to Wilt. Since most of our team was from the poorer sections of the city, we were not accustomed to having fancy dinners. Well, we were invited to a tournament in New York and after the game we had a sit-down dinner with steak as the main course. There was a green leaf on my plate and I didn't know what it was. I asked Jimmy Sadler what it was and he thought that it was parsley, so we both ate it, not knowing it was there for decorative purposes. Everybody started to laugh and you told us to control ourselves or we would have to leave the table. The whole team could not stop laughing and Jimmy and I had to leave. We laughed so much that we were in tears.

Coach, you and the memories are still wonderful to all of us.

—Doug

PART III—GIVING COACHING ANOTHER TRY

My father was a struggling businessman who had, at different times, a butter and egg retail store, a fish market, and a delicatessen in Chester, Pa. The businesses did not last long and this last delicatessen store was failing. My parents were from Europe and sports were not an important event in their lives. I could see that Dad was looking to me for help. He was a gentle, quiet, and non-authoritative figure, especially around my mom who was in charge of everything. My mom was the boss and I could sense each day that things were not going well. Something had to be done or bankruptcy would ensue. Martin, my only brother, was in Germany during the Battle of the Bulge as a medical advisor, so there was no one else to help. I had no alternative but to help. I resigned from the Overbrook position believing full well that my future in education and coaching was gone. This was the hardest thing I had to do in my life. Tears rolled down my face as I sat in my car. I stayed in my father's delicatessen business for three years working seventy-two hours a week, hating every minute. The business started to pick up and fortunately there was a buyer who was interested in purchasing it. My wife kept asking me if this is why I became a teacher and a coach. But I was torn between the obligation to my parents, who were born in Rumania and needed me to run the business, and my future. I took over the business and was the sandwich man also. One day, we were so busy that I turned the sandwich knife upside down when I went to cut the sandwich in half. I was rushed to the hospital for a lot of stitches on many of my fingers. That seemed to be the straw that broke the camel's back. I told my parents that I had to return to coaching and teaching and they seemed to understand. As it turned out, the timing was good and the business was taken over by the purchaser. My relief was overwhelming.

I then started looking around for a job in education while trying to find a coaching position as well. Luckily, I saw an ad in the paper that Upper Moreland High was looking for a coach who also could teach English. I still was not completely certified in English, but hoped that they would consider me. I got an interview with Joe Wesley, who had been a legendary coach at this school before he became the principal, and he immediately hired me. However, I had to take additional English courses to become certified, which I did that summer of 1959.

Joe Wesley

I coached and taught at Upper Moreland for fifteen years with much success and happiness.

I had some very good teams at this school with players who understood the game and were devoted to basketball. The school had a good history of success and with Joe Wesley as the boss, this former coach made certain that the basketball tradition was going to continue.

We usually played a one-three-one zone defense because we had good height. We pressed most of the time, and sometimes played a triangle and two to confuse the other coaches. Most opposing coaches in that league had difficulty trying to set up offenses against these strange defenses. I always tried to vary what my teams were doing and, for the most part, the changes in defense worked. One of my teams, in particular, was very tall and I set the tall players across the foul line and the opposing teams just could not score. That team tied for the championship with a 19–3 record.

I recall one incident that caused me some concern with the principal who hired me. His son, Joe Jr, was on the team and his father would come in to watch the workouts. The first day, he sat quietly on the side bench and just watched. The next day, he became more animated and started to gesture. By the end of the week, he was jumping around coaching vicariously as if he were the coach. I now had a dilemma. What to do? I really loved the guy, but couldn't allow this to continue. I stopped the practice and walked over to him and asked him if we could meet in the stationery closet, which was adjacent to the gym. I then told him in no uncertain terms, but very gently, that as a principal, he was certainly entitled to watch the practices. But, he was not to utter a word if he returned again. He never returned to any of the workouts, although he never missed a game and our relationship never diminished. We did talk about basketball in his office, and he certainly helped me in learning the nuances of the game, which I didn't learn at Overbrook because most of the games were too easy. My time at Upper Moreland was the happiest fifteen years of my educational experience.

I do remember bits and pieces of those many years. Coaches many times get too attached to players. And for obvious reasons, these young athletes emotionally cling onto the coach. I remember one of my young guards who would run through a wall for me if I asked him. His father had been killed in World War II in 1942, when he backed up into a moving propeller of an airplane on an aircraft carrier.

I became this boy's father figure. He was the point guard on a very good team. We won most of our games and shortly after the season tragedy struck. One morning when I was teaching, the football coach, Fred Hoffman, interrupted my class to talk to me. He asked me to come out into the hallway with him. I could see that something was very wrong. He told me that David, my point guard, was racing another car in the street in Hatboro the night before and ran head on into another car and was killed instantly. I was devastated. He was loved by everyone in the school and the funeral was just overwhelming.

David Goldsworthy

Upper Moreland High School 1961
John Rumer, 12, Larry Frank, 13, David Goldsworthy, 11

On a much lighter note, I had two young boys in tenth grade, Joe and John Faulkner, whose father was Henry Faulkner of Faulkner Oldsmobile. They were great kids but uncoordinated and scrawny. They were six foot two or three at the age of fifteen. I kept them on the junior varsity in hopes that one or both of them would help us out two years down the road. They were only allowed, most of the time, to rebound and/or tap the ball against the backboard, hour after hour. They were such good-natured guys that they never complained. As it turned out, as seniors and at six foot five, they were my starting shooting forward and my center on a team that tied for the championship. The father was so thrilled that even though he didn't give me an Oldsmobile, we became dear friends. This was a team that worked hard every day at practice and I just couldn't yell at them. They did everything I asked them to do and they kept me laughing every day in practice. And when it was time to play, they never needed a pep talk.

I can remember the last game of the season with these guys at Central Bucks. We needed to win to tie for the league championship and we were losing by one point with a few seconds to play. My best shooter, Dan Weinberger, was on the foul line for a one and one. Well, he missed the first try, but the shot hit the rim and the rebound came back into his hands and he threw in the winning shot. I nearly fainted. Everybody gathered around me shouting and cheering. I just sat there and couldn't move. It was so emotional.

Joe and John Faulkner.

The faculty members at Upper Moreland were supportive and always came to the games.

The teachers were great as were the students, and I really started to finally become a better English teacher. The student council president that year was a fellow by the name of Jeff Huddleson, who organized a spirit group of students who came out each game to cheer us on while banging on a loud bass drum. He later volunteered to come to my practices and help out where necessary. As it turned out, he later became the varsity coach at Upper Dublin for many years and was the school's most successful coach.

I also learned how to be a better technician at coaching during those years at U.M. since I had to work at all the basic fundamentals and various aspects of coaching these young athletes. This helped to embolden my self-esteem although I wasn't really lacking in confidence. I always knew that I could coach anywhere even without a superstar like Wilt Chamberlain.

However, near the end of my years at Upper Moreland, I felt that I needed to get certified in school administration because the salary was much better and I thought that I could help many more young people as an administrator. I was working nights at the Willow Grove bowling alleys and going to Temple at the same time to get my administrative certification—all while still coaching. My wife and my three young boys would come to the bowling alleys in Willow Grove to have dinner with me, and also so that they could see me once in a while as they were growing up.

REFLECTIONS

Jimmy Buffler 1959–1961 Upper Moreland

I can't tell you how excited I was when I heard that the basketball coach of Wilt Chamberlain was coming to Upper Moreland to coach us in basketball. I was a junior at that time. My first thought always when telling others you coached me is that you were an outstanding teacher of the game and that you always conducted yourself as a gentleman. You taught me how to shoot a jump shot. You gave me personal instructions about the proper technique for shooting a jump shot. I have vivid recollections of these times and how you patiently spent hours and hours helping me. Your only failing is that you couldn't teach me to jump higher (ha ha).

I recall so clearly that in my junior year, you arranged for us to scrimmage Overbrook High School in their tiny gym.

As we walked into the gym, the students who were there to watch the scrimmage wanted to know where our varsity was. Most of our players were less than 6-foot tall and we were small and skinny. I think we had one player who was 6'2.

The scrimmage was so lopsided that their varsity hardly had a workout. Their scrubs did most of the playing. You knew that we were going to get killed, but the teacher in you wanted us to know how basketball was really played. Overbrook, at that time, had Wali Jones, Walt Hazzard, Wayne Hightower, Ralph Hayward, and a few other stars that I can't remember. You told us that that this experience would make us better players and a better team sometime down the road. And it did.

I went to your summer camp, Camp Pinecrest, with a few of our players and the Darby team was there also. It was at your camp that I decided that I wanted to go to college. My mother was a widow, and we did not have the finances to send me to college. My only alternative was to try to get a scholarship to college.

During my senior year, I scored 55 points in one game against Souderton High School and scored a total of 970 some points in my career. The 55-point game was in all the newspapers and I was interviewed by our local newspaper. It was an exciting time for me. I credit my success to you and the time and patience you spent with me.

As you know, I received a full four-year scholarship to American University. I attended all 4 years at the college and graduated in 1965. I was the co-captain of the basketball team my senior year.

My memories of my playing time at Upper Moreland live with me forever. Thanks to you, coach.

—Jimmy

REFLECTIONS

George (Buddy) Watts 1960–1961 Upper Moreland

I remember a coach who took a bratty, wise-guy kid and taught him to be accountable and to accept responsibility. He made that kid into a good student citizen and a contributing member of a team. That kid, of course, was me. Because of your efforts, I matured overnight and gained the respect of my teachers and classmates. On one magical night, I scored 32 points against Souderton and Jimmy scored over 30 points also that night. I didn't know how many points I scored that night. It wasn't until at school that next day that I found out when I was walking down the halls. Everybody was saying "hello" and offering congratulations. I felt very special ... an important commodity in a school community. Thank goodness you didn't let it go to my head. You made sure of that by being harder on me than anyone else that next day in practice. You also taught me to love and respect the game of basketball and constantly encouraged me to shoot the ball (the only aspect of the game that I did well). But, because I shot the ball so much, my teammates were always angry with me for not passing the ball. Then when I went into the navy and made the ship's team and scored 40 points in the first game, these sailor teammates also got mad at me for not passing the ball. Following the stint in the navy, I wanted to stay close to basketball. I became a referee for thirty-five years. I worked the state finals at the high school level, Division I championship games, plus NCAA tournaments at the college level...all because you got me to love the game so much. Because of your efforts, you have made me an honest and respected person, a loving father, and husband. My family thanks you for that. You even impacted my life twenty years later. One day I went with my daughter to see an Upper Moreland game. You had a pretty good team and were in the playoffs. I took Megan to the game. She was only ten years old. After the game, we hugged and I introduced her to you and told her who you were. Your response was, "Meg, your father was one of my greatest players." I really wasn't, of course, but Meg was so proud of her father that she talked about it for days. Again, thank you for changing my life in so many positive ways.

You will always be my hero.

—Buddy

REFLECTIONS

Joe Wesley Jr. 1962–1964 Upper Moreland

I will never forget you coming over to David Goldsworthy and me when we were in ninth grade and telling us that you thought that we could start on the varsity as sophomores. After that day, I thought of nothing else but playing for the team in tenth grade.

I remember my first game. I was probably more nervous than the other players. It was my first start although the other team members had played six games. I had been hurt in football and I was not ready to play for a month. I was awful that night. I thought that I had blown my chances to ever start again. However, you put me right back in the starting position the very next game and I played much better. I started to play better each game knowing that you had confidence in me. You said that I was going to be a player. I knew at that moment that I wanted to be a teacher, a coach, and maybe some day I would make a young player feel the same way as I did. The 1963–64 Golden Bears was one of the best teams that Upper Moreland ever had (including my father's teams when he coached years ago). We won nineteen games and lost one. One was a four-overtime thriller that was stolen from us by the official. I will never forget the last eight seconds when we came up with a steal, and the other guard and I were on a 2-on-1 fast break. Just above the foul line, Jimmy, the other guard, passed me the ball and I tipped it back to him. The defender was so faked out by the two quick passes that he tripped and fell to the floor. And Jimmy took the ball and gently laid it into the basket. As the ball fell through the basket, the buzzer sounded that ended the game. Everyone ran out onto the court shouting and cheering. We thought that we had scored an incredible victory. No one heard the whistle blow and Jimmy was called for walking. We lost by 1 point. We did get revenge two weeks later by beating them by thirty points. You and the game of basketball gave me so much confidence and self-assuredness. I was taught more about sacrifice, dedication, leadership, and teamwork than any classroom ever could.

After college, I went on to coach the boys' varsity at Lower Moreland for seven years and then coached the girls' varsity at the same school for nine years, winning championships the last four years. I later coached at Wissahicken for three years, winning championships the last two years. I also later coached at Abington for six years, winning the championship the last year. Over my career, I know that I won over 400 games. Along the way, I continued to do what you did with me by encouraging players by giving pats on my players' backs and supportive words to them, which, I hope, made my players feel the way you made me feel.

Thanks for everything. I will never forget you.

—Joe Jr.

Feb. 15, 1998

Dear Coach,

Congratulations on an outstanding career in coaching. There sure are a lot of individuals who are better players and better people because of you and I'm one of them. You have always been a special person to me as my teacher, student council advisor, and role model in coaching. You have always provided me with support and encouragement. You have been an inspiration to me and have helped me be a better teacher and coach than I ever would have been without you.

Thank you so much for all you have done for me. You should be proud of your accomplishments in teaching and coaching. I know that I am very proud of you and feel fortunate to have been able to get to know you and share some wonderful times with you.

Sincerely,
Jeff Huddleston
Upper Dublin Basketball coach

PART IV—MY YEARS AS A JUNIOR HIGH PRINCIPAL

When I finally became certified, I served as an assistant principal in Upper Moreland High School for one year and then at William Tennent for one year before I applied to Tredyffrin/Easttown School District. I never taught in a junior high school, but the prospects of being successfully interviewed seemed good, since I was well known around the suburban area for my coaching. I got an interview with the superintendent and his two assistants. Luckily for me, all three knew of my background and that I had coached Wilt. The aura of coaching Wilt followed me all through my life. I believe that the deciding factors were that my reputation at Overbrook preceded me, along with my resume and favorable comments by my friends who were also faculty members.

I was appointed by the school board and was told by the superintendent that the school was in perfect shape as far as the staff's professionalism was concerned, and the students were getting a superior education.

But then again, maybe not so superior.

My first faculty meeting was a nightmare.

A group of male teachers sat on the back, right side of the conference room and all the female teachers sat in the front middle. I was excited because this was my first exposure to my staff as a principal. I stood in the center with my notes on the lectern, expecting everyone to get quiet. The female staff members were courteous, but the "boys" in the right rear never stopped talking, nor did they acknowledge that I was waiting for them to get quiet. There was one very outspoken faculty member whose name was Peter Snipe whom I got to know very well later on, unfortunately.

I yelled "hello" a few times and asked for their attention so that I could introduce myself. They started to quiet down slowly, and I began by telling them about my plans, aspirations, and goals that I hoped we could accomplish together. I talked for about ten minutes, but I felt that I was alone in this very large room. As a speaker, one knows when the audience is with him. I was uncomfortable. I felt nothing. The kibitzing began again as I continued my remarks; I intuitively knew that they were not listening to a word I was saying. I needed to gain control of the situation quickly. But how? I couldn't reprimand them on my first meeting and I couldn't show them that I was becoming upset with their behavior—or could I? I had seen this behavior the day before in a section of the faculty lunchroom called the "pit."

I tried to remain calm and composed and in a non-threatening few words managed to regain their attention. I was rather ill at ease, and I could feel beads of sweat running down my back as my under-shirt became wet with perspiration. At that instant, I realized that my task as an educational leader of this school would not be a pleasant one, nor as simple as I had envisioned. I made some mental notes about the lineup of the boys and tried to connect faces with names. I later observed that these were the same male faculty members who always ate together in one section of the faculty lunchroom where no female staff member dared sit near for fear of ridicule and/or verbal abuse. The laughing and foul language that came from that section of the lunchroom were appalling and completely devoid of professionalism, as was my very first faculty meeting.

As time went on, I had to deal with the most obnoxious situations with these male staff members. At various times, I would find a male teacher sleep-ing in a class room, calling students "bucket bottom" or "scumbag" or other devastating nick names, or not teaching the required curriculum. They continually undermined innovative ideas and/or programs. Sex-ual mind games were played with the ninth grade students frequently. But in spite of all these obstacles, our school, years later, was recognized for having outstanding model programs for the mentally retarded and for innovative accelerated programs for gifted students. We received international acclaim highlighted by being on the front page of the Wall Street Journal, and we were honored to receive the National Award for Excellence, in the Rose Garden with President Ronald Reagan.

THE BROWNIE CAPER

I did have some laughs in between the miseries of being a principal. I inherited an elderly white-haired Irish battle-ax secretary who was responsible for the finances of the school. She let me know in no uncertain terms that she didn't want any part of the faculty and I had better keep them away from her. She bullied them and that was that. I later found out that the staff felt the same way about her. She also told me that she didn't like ethnic groups or minorities. But I was OK. She was very outspoken and intimidated everyone for more years than anyone cared to remember. I was relieved to learn that she was going to retire in December of the second year. All I needed to do was to stay out of her way for a few more months. I hired Rosie to replace the elderly lady. Rosie had been working at the district office for a few years and was eager to make a change. She wanted to be around young people and had a real love for the students. She was a scout leader and had a wonderful relationship with the young girls in the community. Her secretarial skills were excellent, although I was told that she was somewhat different. She was willing to take chances. Some days she would come in dressed as a clown. Other days she was Charlie Chaplin (see picture). Occasionally she brought her duck to school or her gerbils, and sometimes, she brought a couple of her cats. More often than not, she made cookies or pastries for the office workers and was willing to help out whenever she was needed. If I could have hired her as a public relations circus person rather than a secretary, she would have been in ecstasy. Rosie was about thirty-five years old at that time and her prime interest in life was being queen mother to the girl scouts and nurturing her many pets. In addition to her duck, her gerbils, and cats, she also had a lamb, a goat, and a few dogs. Her mother and father were elderly folks and Rosie cared for them reverently on their small farm. When the goat died a few years later, Rosie tried to get two bereavement days from the school district for mourning. She was turned down and almost quit because of this. I had to plead with her to stay on the job.

One day, I mentioned to her that sandwiches had been disappearing from the faculty dining room refrigerator and we couldn't seem to find out who was taking the sandwiches. Rosie suggested a plan of attack.

She would make a batch of brownies laced with ex-lax and hot peppers. We would leave the brownies in the refrigerator overnight and observe carefully for the next few days. For two days, the brownies in a wrapped package remained untouched and we were becoming discouraged. On the third day, the brownies disappeared at approximately 10 in the morning. This was the scheduled time that the middle shift of custodians arrived. About three hours later, one of the custodians called the main office complaining of a terrible stomachache and that he was going to leave work. I asked the lead custodian what was the matter with Charlie and was told that he had eaten some brownies that had been in the refrigerator and he got sick.

The next day I had a decorated cake for Rosie with a blue ribbon attached and a note congratulating her for her successful sleuthing. After that episode, nothing else was ever missing from the refrigerator.

Rosie

THE TURNING POINT
AT THIS SCHOOL

As the years passed, I continued to feel frustrated and a tremendous sense of urgency to talk to someone in central administration as a result of my many misgivings about certain factions of the faculty. The superintendent always seemed too busy to see me because I think he couldn't deal with my school problems, so I always saw the second-in-command, his assistant, Mr. Weston Cartwright. Wes was a pencil pusher, who spent most of his time sitting at his desk writing reports for the school board and putting out fires for the superintendent. Rarely was he out of his office; therefore, all of the information that was gathered was once removed from the original source. Mr. Cartwright's primary interest in life was watching ESPN and talking about sports. That was my entry level into his inner circle of friends. If one could talk about the world of sports, then one could get an attentive ear. I explained the many problems that I was encountering. He listened politely, but I sensed that he did not hear or want to hear what I was saying. He indicated that he would talk to the superintendent and get back to me in a few days. Perhaps, I didn't explain my case effectively. I got no response for the next ten days. Sensing that Mr. Cartwright had not relayed my problems to the superintendent or that they had chosen to ignore them, I decided to write a detailed memo to Dr. Harvard, the superintendent. I told him that the school was about to explode, that morale seemed to be at a low, and I desperately needed support from central administration. I told him that my assistant principal was undermining my every move. (He originally applied for the principal's position and was ignored.) I told him that there were serious academic problems and that very questionable morals existed among selected staff members. I sent him documented information for all of these items. I never received one response, nor was I asked to meet with him to discuss the events that were troubling me. I became resigned to the fact that I was going to battle these problems alone and, down the road, I could be in deep trouble without district support. I kept reassuring myself that I had to continue on the course I had chosen. I was not willing to compromise my philosophy about kids and education. The situation did not get better the next few months and every day was emotionally troubling. On one late afternoon that I will never forget, I was handed a cryptic note from one of my loyal teachers informing me that the leaders of my adversarial group were organizing a clandestine faculty meeting. The meeting was going to be held late in the afternoon without any administrators. All those individuals who were unhappy with me and sympathetic to their cause were encouraged to submit a list of grievances to the leader of the adversarial group, Mr. Peter Snipe. Most of the staff members attended. Many were just curious and innocent listeners. I was led to believe that there were heated arguments on both sides of the aisle, but in the end, the antagonists prevailed. Their bullying tactics beat down what opposition. Teachers are usually somewhat docile, and non-confrontational. They want to stay in their classrooms, mind their own business, and just teach.

I hastily put in a conference call to Dr. Harvard and insisted that he talk to me immediately, regardless of his schedule.

I now felt that I had his attention. He cautioned me to go about my business and that he now realized the gravity of the situation. I will never forget my feelings during the next forty-eight hours. My world was crumbling and I thought that I might not survive this crisis. My job was in jeopardy and my confidence was dramatically slipping. The next day, Snipe came into my office as brazen as ever and told me that the faculty had decided that I should be replaced as principal as soon as possible. I shall never forget that meeting as he smugly sat back in his chair in my office, apparently in absolute control of my future. Mr. Snipe was an officer of the teachers' union in the district, so he felt that he had the authority to relay this message to me.

He was the teacher who was my prime opponent in my quest to turn this school around. Here was a person who stood for everything I loathed in a professional telling me that I was going to lose my job. He even called the superintendent to inform him of the faculty meeting. The superintendent finally called me over to his office that afternoon so I could tell him the series of events that led to this meeting and what I had done to avoid this crisis. I couldn't believe my ears. After he had told me that the school was perfect when he hired me, he finally was pulling his head out of the sand. I again told him as bluntly as I could that Snipe and a few other staff members were corrupting the morals of the children and I gave him dozens of examples. I did not endear myself to him at the meeting. I left the meeting emotionally drained. He told me that he would get back to me within twenty-four hours. I couldn't read his mind nor could I imagine what his next step would be. I had never been anything but successful in my career and here I was on the verge of losing my job. My stomach was churning and I couldn't hold any food in me. I went home and told my wife that I was about to get fired. I had no doubt that the ugly enemy would prevail and that Snipe would gloat to his buddies how he was responsible for my downfall. I received a call the next morning from Dr. Harvard. He was considering many options; however, before any decision would be made, he was going to conduct a thorough investigation by speaking to every member of the faculty. During the next two days, three central administrators would conduct the investigation.

The next morning at seven, the three administrators arrived. The staff had been told that they would be conducting some private interviews with them. At the end of the day, they left the building without talking to me. Needless to say, the day was not pleasant. Every nerve in my body was tingling. I was depressed and the uncertainty about what was going to happen was killing me. I was brain-dead. I went home and tried to keep busy. I cut the lawn and fixed things around the house and worried and worried and worried. If I lost my job, how could I pay my bills and my mortgage? But I still was not going to compromise my principles. The students were getting cheated and I was not going to let them down. I was in my office at six that next morning. I couldn't sleep so there was no reason to stay home and drive my wife crazy. I got a call from the superintendent. He and the other administrators were coming over after lunch and that I was supposed to let the staff know that there would be a faculty meeting that afternoon. The meeting with the staff lasted about forty-five minutes. I was not invited to the meeting. It seemed like an eternity to me. After the meeting the superintendent came into my office without the other administrators. He started out by saying that I was not going to be replaced as principal. What an emotional release I had, although I suspected that he didn't realize it. He told me that there had been overwhelming support for what I was trying to accomplish and that the small group of hostile staff members had organized a lynch mob. The silent majority had come to my rescue. Staff members who had been reluctant to speak came forward and supported my efforts. The superintendent told me that my assistant principal was a part of that group and was the instigator for many of the selective leaks and gross misrepresentations, and the assistant was going to be transferred out of my school. He shook my hand and left the office.

As luck would have it, Mr. Snipe later became preoccupied with marital problems. His wife had finally had it with him and his antics. He was distracted with divorce proceedings. He bothered me little those last few months and I suspect that he had a serious talk with Dr. Harvard shortly after our meeting.

I almost got fired again a few years later and this time I was feeling no pain. I have had chronic back problems for years that flared up from time to time. Because of athletic abuse, my spinal discs are somewhat degenerated and when I exercise too vigorously, the nerves become irritated and the sciatic nerve does a number on me. I really am in terrible pain and I need to lie on my back to get relief. The pain shoots down my right leg and I can't bend forward to reach my toes. In fact, I can barely reach my knees. This condition cropped up a few years later after that terrible time with the superintendent.

And it was most serious when it was time for my annual evaluation with Dr Harvard and Mr. Cartwright. The evaluation, in reality, was somewhat of a farce. It was always written by an assistant to the superintendent and it was usually based on hearsay and comments made by various people throughout the school year. I was somewhat concerned that one of the statements in the evaluation dealt with what I considered a minor oversight on my part. A few months earlier, I had been sent to Atlanta, Georgia, to attend a conference as a last-minute replacement for the other junior high principal who suddenly resigned from the district. In my haste to accommodate the superintendent's request, I forgot to initial the time cards for the custodial staff. No one other than the principal was permitted to sign the cards on orders from the personnel department. Therefore, the custodial staff was not going to get paid because I had to personally verify that they had worked the hours stated on the time cards. The superintendent called me at the convention in Georgia and I had to confirm to him that each card was correct and that it was OK for him to sign them. I sensed that this item was going to show up on my final evaluation and I was prepared to dispute its ridiculous inclusion. My back was killing me on the day of the evaluation, so I took three Percodan pills to get me through the day. One of my secretaries liked to play nurse and gave me a handful of these painkillers in case I needed relief from pain, since she knew that I was having a problem. I tried to get dressed that morning, but I couldn't put my shoes and socks on my feet. The beads of sweat were running down my face and I was having terrible chills, but I was determined to get to the evaluation. I made it to the car at eleven o'clock that morning, but I couldn't sit upright because of the pain. I moved the seat from the traditional 90-

degree angle to an angle of 135 degrees, so that I was almost prone with my right leg limp on the gas pedal. I braked with my left foot. I remember that when I stopped for a red light, the people in the next car stared at me. They must have questioned how I could drive with my head in such a laid-back position. The occupants in the car surely wondered how I could drive with such a deformity. I made it to the school in a suit that was drenched with sweat and with a pair of moccasins next to me on the seat. Inside the moccasins were my socks. My secretary took one look at me and rushed to help me into my office before anyone could see me. I asked her if she would put on my socks and moccasins. I then told her I was ready to meet with the superintendent.

About this time the Percodan pills were working and I really didn't know where I was or what I was doing. I was feeling no pain and my vocabulary had no constraints. Dr. Harvard and his assistant arrived about fifteen minutes later and started to talk about the school year and my evaluation. I don't precisely remember what I said after I read the evaluation, but I do remember reading a statement about those stupid time cards and then everything went blank. I was told subsequently by Wes that I yelled at the boss for about fifteen minutes and that all my pent-up feelings over these past many years just poured out. I signed the evaluation and went to a faculty meeting that I had previously scheduled and I was told that I was not very pleasant at that meeting also. That next day, Dr. Harvard summoned me to his office. I knew that I was in trouble again. He informed me that he was in the process of writing me up for insubordination as a result of our meeting that previous day, but he had been told by his assistant that I had been heavily sedated. He said that he was willing to forget the whole ugly episode and remove that item concerning the time cards. He did admit that what I had said and all of the previous conversations with him made him finally fully understand what I had been going through these many years. He conceded that he would listen more carefully to what I had to say. I now knew that my time as principal of this school was nearing an end. I was weary of the constant battles and realized that I was emotionally worn out. The turbulent years had taken their toll on me. However, I wanted to stay just a little longer to apply for the National Award for Excellence in Education.

With the help of special faculty members, we started to accomplish my goals in the school and subsequently, a special invitation to the Rose Garden with the president of the United States absolutely solidified my resolve.

TALK ABOUT COURAGE

Some time near the end of my tenure at the school, a wonderful social studies teacher and good friend came in to see me before school opened in August. I

had admired Karl for his personal courage in fighting cancer and for his excellence in the classroom,
and he knew how I felt about him. Our relationship
was excellent. He had observed the anguish I had
endured over these many years and although he was
non-confrontational with that other group, he said
what he had to say when the situation warranted it.
Karl had a pallid complexion and looked thin and
emotionally wiped out. Enrollment was down and
the school district was moving toward the concept of
an intermediate school. Sixth grade was going to be
included in the organizational setup in addition to
the seventh and eighth grades. He had been working all summer planning for this change. But this
was not why he stopped in to see me at this time.

Karl began the conversation by telling me that
he was proud to have known me all these years. He
went on talking about things that had bothered
him concerning education and the profession. He
said that he was going to give me a note that he had
written and asked me to read it after he left. His
eyes were misty. We embraced and, for some reason,
I couldn't hold back my tears. Our emotions were
high and I sensed all was not well. He always began
his notes to me with,

August, 1986
Dear friend,
    We have been together for many years,
and I want you to know that your support,
your kindness, and your professionalism

have constantly amazed me and com-
forted me. Your strength to stand tall in
the face of adversity is something I could
not have handled. That year when everything was at a very low ebb amid the tur-
moil and misunderstandings, I wondered
how you were going to react and survive,
and I wondered how I would have reacted
if I were in your shoes. You not only came
out fighting—I would have given up—but
you put negativism aside and maintained
a positive approach to the rest of us who
stood idly by. You personally have made
this school something that we can all be
proud of and have moved us to greater
accomplishments.

I learned an important lesson from
watching the whole progression of events
during those awful first few years. I should
have been much more vocal and stron-
ger and supported you much more vigorously, but I didn't have the courage, nor
the inner strength that you had. A lesser
person would have quit long ago. You have
supporters on this staff who have gathered strength from your leadership and are
beginning to stand tall to your detractors.
The battle is not over, but the tide is beginning to dramatically turn in your favor.

I need to tell you one more thing. My
cancer has spread. I need to go in for more

surgery. I wish to keep this confidential for as long as I can.

Your good friend, Karl

There are tiers of courage and each level is important, but little compares with the courage of this man.
His prognosis was not good.

That next year we received the National Award for Excellence. The parents became very involved and we were selected through the tireless efforts of my friend, Karl, who was very sick, and by staff members who worked hard to achieve this wonderful tribute and recognition, although a few years earlier it was the impossible dream.

OCTOBER, 1987 ROSE GARDEN, WASHINGTON. D.C.

"Ladies and Gentlemen, the President of the United States."

We all rose and looked to our left.

In strode President Ronald Reagan looking tan and fit, dressed splendidly in a light-brown finely tailored suit. He walked briskly to the lectern. Accompanying him was William Bennett, the United States Secretary of Education.

I was sitting in the first row of chairs facing the president. This was the famed Rose Garden. I was one of 220 proud principals invited as guests of the president and the United States Department of Education. We were being honored as recipients of the National Award for Excellence. Our junior high had been selected from among thousands of elementary and junior high schools as worthy of this prestigious award. What a proud and exhilarating moment!

As I looked around, I could see security guards stationed on the roof and in every corner of the Rose Garden. In the rear of the Rose Garden were hundreds of photographers and members of the press corps. The ceremony lasted about twenty minutes. After the ceremony was over, Sam Donaldson began shouting, "Mr. President, Mr. President, What about the Bork nomination? What about the Bork nomination?"

This was a hot political issue, but the timing of his shouting seemed inappropriate at this ceremony. Judge Bork had been nominated for the United States Supreme Court position and was being denied this opportunity by Congress. The president didn't respond and abruptly walked out of the Rose Garden. Donaldson received considerable TV coverage for his unexpected outburst at this ceremony and since I was near him, my face was also on national television.

After this outburst, all of the reporters and Mr. Donaldson gathered around the principals to discuss their schools and their special programs for which we were selected for this wonderful recognition. I exited proudly with my wife, some excited parents, and selected teachers who accompanied me to Washington.

When I retired one year later I wrote a book about the school and the horrendous experiences that I encountered with these staff members entitled *Mr. Principal, Your Activity Period Sucks*. The title of the book came about as a result of a private meeting that I had with Mr. Snipe, my main adversary for many years, who happened to be an executive officer of the teacher's association. He accused me of scheduling an activity period each day for the students and that interfered with some of the teacher's unscheduled time. He wrote to me and told me that the activity period "sucked."

I leaned back in my chair in my office and thought how to respond. I wasn't certain what had inspired him to write that note to me, but I did know that it represented to me a monumental concern; not only for whomever he represented, but also for me at this stage in my tenure. He sent this note to guarantee a confrontation. I decided to face him head on. I called him in to my office and as the meeting progressed, I told him I received his note and that he could have said,

"Mr. Principal, Your Activity Lacks Creativity, The Program is Hopeless, Futile, Impossible, Past Hope, Irretrievable, Irreparable, Beyond Remedy, Gloomy, Dismal, Disquieting, Intimidating,

Demoralizing, Unnerving, Direful, Ghastly, Morbid, Gross.

But you chose to use the word, 'sucks,' which is certainly somewhat beneath educational standards."
I was emotionally upset although I would not let him know and I could feel my heart beating as if it were coming out of my chest and ready to explode. I was angry and I sensed that his uneasiness was considerable. He was looking to explore a weakness in my psyche, but former coaches can always weather storms like this. He was hoping that I would back down. Fortunately, I knew that the staff was happy with the activity period and voiced strong approval. This was a victory for me, but I continued to watch my back.

I ended the meeting abruptly after I told him that there would be no change in the activity period.

I could hear all of my office help laughing hysterically outside of my office.

Thank God for my thesaurus.

My book was published shortly afterward and there was a lot of publicity in Philadelphia about it, especially in the Upper Main Line surroundings. A short time later, I received a call from the producer of the Sally Jesse Raphael show asking me if I would be a guest on her show. Without hesitation, I jumped at the chance to promote my book.

The day of the show arrived and I was sitting in the "green" room with another principal by the name of Joe Clark.

A movie was written and produced about him

entitled *Lean On Me,* a story about his antics of roaming around in the hallways in a high school using a bullhorn. We spoke for a while and then we were introduced to the audience. I thought that I was invited to talk about my book. Little did I know that I was going to be a patsy in the program, so that the other principal, Joe Clark, would look good in the eyes of the audience. And I, the suburban principal would look like I had a plush job with no discipline problems. Certain people in the audience had little stickers on their shirts and blouses and Sally mysteriously gravitated to them to ask them specific questions. They attacked me verbally and made the other principal look good. I held my ground and came out of it alive. I even had a chance to talk about my book for a few minutes on the show, much to Sally's chagrin. After the show, I told the producer in no uncertain terms what I thought of her and Sally. Before I left the studio, Joe Clark came up to me and apologized. He ended with, "You and I ought to go on tour; we would make a good team."

PART V—THE TOUGHEST CHALLENGE IN MY COACHING CAREER

The one constant quality about all basketball coaches is that they are dreamers.

Coaches take immense pride in helping all players develop and get them to achieve their potential. They hope to make players better than they were. But as dreamers, coaches envision transforming all players through their tireless efforts of varying psychologies into the Michael Jordans and the Wilt Chamberlains of the world. However, coaches many times disregard the realities of a player's limitations and physical inadequacies. In addition, their dreams propel them to levels of unreachable heights, engaging, for the most part, in unattainable goals.

I was that kind of dreamer even before I coached Wilt Chamberlain, whose presence led me to successes far beyond my wildest dreams. Coaching Wilt and basketball during those wonderful years at Overbrook High in the fifties were legendary, but I now needed to get back to what I loved the most—coaching.

A year later, after I resigned from the principal's position, I applied at William Tennent High School. They were looking for a coach. Tennent had a history of a strong musical program and, conversely, a dismal athletic program with a lack of interest in basketball. I clearly knew what the challenges were.

But what did that matter? I coached the best player in the world. I could win anywhere. All I needed was a group of aspiring young men who wanted to play basketball and I certainly could mold them into a winning team—no matter what the opposition. At least that's what I told myself.

I was hired for the coaching position almost immediately.

THE BEGINNING, 1975

I held my first meeting in October with those students who were going to try out for the team. It was here that I would outline out my plans for the coming season, the practice schedules, and what we needed in order to transform this school into a basketball powerhouse in the Suburban I League. This league traditionally was one of the strongest suburban leagues in the state of Pennsylvania. The room filled up quickly with starry-eyed youngsters filled with enthusiasm.

Visibly absent were African Americans and players not much taller than six feet.

My individual contacts with the varsity players revealed a myriad of excuses from them that gave me an uneasy feeling that things were going to be very difficult for a long period of time.

November 15th was the starting date for tryouts. I had been warned by the athletic director that cuts should not be made for, at least, four days since parents probably could question my decisions through the school administrators.

I knew after ten minutes who could play, and who had potential. Nicholas was one of the players who caught my eye immediately. He was short, quiet, and had an innocent look about him. His basketball skills were just awful. He ran with a waddle and his large feet pointed outward like a quarter of two on the face of a clock. He shot lay ups off the wrong foot, which in basketball is a major mistake in the art of the game and made every shot look awkward and unsightly. Before we were able to cut him, he went out and bought himself a pair of sneakers that cost a great deal of money. They appeared to be "the state of the art" sneakers. He did not make the team that year

Fast forward to the following year. He arrived again to try out for the team. He was three inches taller but still had the same weaknesses. He became somewhat of a caricature with the other players, someone with whom they felt sorry for but at whom they continuously laughed.

I just couldn't cut him again.

We kept him on the junior varsity and occasionally he got into a game. He got a junior varsity letter that year and that was the end of his career. I subsequently received a letter from his father who was a chemical engineer from a prestigious university thanking me and our program for building up his self-confidence so that he no longer was the insecure, introverted youngster that haunted him all of his life. We never know how our decisions affect the psyche of impressionable young men.

I kept the tryouts going for four interminable days. Last year's varsity players were excused from trying out although it appeared to me that there wasn't much separation of abilities from those on the court and the "varsity players." The previous year's record was two wins and twenty losses.

I knew that the problems were enormous, the chances for success overwhelmingly against us, the psychological barriers horrendous. The school's student body was primarily a white middle-class group of students for whom athletics were not a priority. Participating in the concert band or the marching band or the debating club were higher priorities for these youngsters. A priority did exist with a small number of parents who had some personal experience in sports, who envisioned their youngsters as having some athletic ability, or who were living vicariously through their own participation in athletics. Many of the aspirants who tried out for the team were lacking in skills and, for the most part, less athletic than at the other schools in the conference.

Where does one begin to put all of the pieces together? How could I ever overcome the stigma of losing? I was just twenty-two years old when I inherited Wilt Chamberlain and a supporting cast of players who had been tagged by many basketball mavens as the best high school team ever to play in Pennsylvania. We were virtually unbeatable. For the most part, the margin of winning exceeded forty points a game. This was so different.

THE LAST BUS RIDE HOME
THAT FIRST YEAR

The windows were all steamed up from the players' bodies. For the first time this year, the bus ride home was unusually quiet, with reflections of images, and unfulfilled hopes and dreams drifting in the minds of the players. When we arrived back at the school, I watched each player disappear with hugs, with handshakes, with good-byes. Adam was the last one to leave the bus. The coaches always got off first to talk to the guys, to commiserate, to encourage, and to thank them for their efforts. This was the last game of a disastrous season. We had only won a few games. The boys quickly disappeared into the darkness of the night with the exception of Adam. I could see Adam's shoulders slightly slumped over so that his 6'4" frame belied his stature. He looked puny and insignificant as the rain peppered his leather jacket. The fog seemed to engulf his very being. It was finally over. He was the last player to leave the bus as everyone ran quickly to their cars. He stood motionless, seemingly incapable or perhaps just hesitant to move forward to his waiting father. The long, endless disappointing season had finally ended and yet, Adam stood with tears in his eyes, unwilling to accept the finality of it all.

Adam was a senior in this tortured basketball program who had envisions of changing this world of ours. He was full of excitement and enthusiasm, truly believing in himself and his athletic peers. However, in athletics, there are only peaks and valleys and the valleys far outnumbered the peaks. This season was endless, the practices unyielding, and the losses more and more difficult to accept. Yet, each new day had brought renewed enthusiasm and hope. Now it was over.

Adam was a somewhat raw-boned youngster with a high energy level. He lacked certain skills, but survived because of an intense desire to succeed. This drive caught my attention. He would dive for loose balls; he would be the first back on defense; he would take charges until his body ached. The bruises on his body and the lack of oxygen never seemed to get in the way of his desire to achieve and to please.

Adam played sparingly throughout the early part of the season, but somewhere near the latter part of the season, he had one game that was remarkable. Not only did he rebound well, which was one of his strong points, but he scored fifteen points and helped the team pull off a rare, stunning upset. His father, who was extremely vocal in a negative sense, always sat just behind the coaches' bench. He constantly berated everyone and everything about this team and probably directed his remarks at his son and me for both not living up to his expectations. In the father's mind, this game vindicated him and his beliefs. His son deserved more playing time and this game proved it. The coaches were incompetent and poor judges of talent. Unfortunately, Adam never played another good game and the father's tirades were even louder and more specifically directed at his son for all of the fans to hear. The embarrassment was overwhelming and their relationship suffered, although never in public.

As I approached Adam in the darkness of the night, he began to sob uncontrollably. I tried to console him but with little success. He finally turned, stood a little straighter and quietly, but with strength in his voice said,

"Even through the anguish that my father caused, I never wanted it to end. I loved every minute, even with the disappointments, the embarrassments, the endless valleys, and that one peak that will live with me forever."

PREPARING A TEAM FOR COMBAT

The preparation of a basketball team is an overwhelming job even when the players are skilled. The many facets of individual and team basketball are so intensely intricate that it takes years, prior to the high school age, for a youngster to just learn skills and techniques that would allow him or her to compete at a varsity level. However, the acquisition of skills is not enough. The competition factor under game conditions is another part of the formula. The inner-city kids have the advantage of competing with players of different abilities. Their combative toughness is developed at a much earlier age. Any community center in the Philadelphia area will always have basketball games going on at all hours of the day and, more often than not, long into the hours of the night. The basketball season is twelve months long for the inner city players and, at that time, the suburban player played four months of basketball and participated in other sports as well. The availability of competition at a high level is always present for the city kid. The suburban player does not have access to this type of constant competition. Although it is less true today, much time was spent practicing in the driveway or in pickup games against like abilities. This type of player was not aware of the layers of competencies. The truly dedicated player takes the initiative to play outside of his circle and compete in areas where the level of competition is far greater than his neighborhood.

The kids who make the team are enthusiastic, resilient, hard workers, and courteous. They are like sponges, absorbing every little detail, and every little nuance, undaunted in their excitement to participate at the varsity level, naive about the battles that they would have to endure, and the heartbreak that would accompany the many losses.

Psychologically, they not only have to play against superior teams in a monstrous conference with highly skilled players, but against opposing players who have started at a higher level of confidence. Other teams are aware that they are playing against a school team whose success rate has been suspect for a number of years.

Crashing through these emotional barriers greatly exacerbated the task of this underdog.

One of those early years, early in the season, we lost to Norristown High School by eighty points. The other coach never stopped pressing the whole game. I said to myself as I walked out to the waiting bus,

"Don't ever forget this embarrassment. Someday, you will get a chance to return this favor."

My wife stopped coming to the games because she couldn't stand to see the anguish on my face. I came home after each game and reported that we lost by thirty points or more. Shortly afterward, she stopped asking me about the games and we sort of stopped talking about basketball around the house that first year.

ONE VERY TALENTED, TROUBLED PLAYER

John, so far, was the most talented player I had at this school. This was the second year. Playing his last game as a junior, he scored twenty-four points and because his innate skills were so strong, we were projecting him to possibly be an all-league candidate his senior year, providing he could overcome his horrendous emotional problems. As a junior, he had a miserable season for the most part and drove me to distraction. I compromised all of my coaching philosophies to accommodate his personal needs, unfortunately at the expense of the team's unity and morale.

When the season began, John was not on the team because of his many distractions that included personal depression, suicidal tendencies, and an obsessive infatuation with a young girl that kept him emotionally paralyzed. He did join the team three weeks after practice had started. After much consultation with his counselor and the administration, I was convinced that keeping him on the team was the right thing to do, although I had much trepidation. This was my first compromise with this young man. As the season progressed, he missed practices because of various excuses and missing practices was the beginning of a creeping cancer to the team's unity. He missed the Christmas tournament, claiming that he didn't know that we had games scheduled over the holiday season, and he continually missed the bus for away games. As the ulcers were expanding in my stomach, I knew that I was violating my own principles, anguishing between right and wrong. I knew full well that it was wrong for the good of the team, but probably right for him as a human being. In my earlier years as a coach, the absolute good of the team came first, but as I matured, I felt a compulsion to "save" this young man if possible, if the sacrifice was not too imposing on the team.

As the season progressed, he began to adhere to the rules and was visibly better able to handle his distractions. He became a team player and his season culminated in that outstanding last game. His senior year did not live up to my expectations, but he was a team player who violated no rules. The gamble of last year seemed to pay off. Although his personal basketball ambitions were disappointing, his personal life moved in a more positive direction.

I have seen him recently. He is married and has a good job and his memories of that special season were relayed to me with a "thank you," a warm handshake, and a close embrace.

Sometimes, even though we anguish at our own

rigidity, we are rewarded quietly by our personal convictions.

However, there are times when the athlete does not respond to coaching authority as a result of his temperament or upbringing.

Mike was a junior varsity fringe player and his coach, Jim, was the varsity football coach as well as the JV basketball coach. Jim was a no nonsense guy but fair to all of the players. During one of the practice sessions Jim was correcting Mike of some flawed technique. Mike, who was an African American, yelled "Man, who the bleep are you talking to? You have no bleeping right to talk to me," and stormed off the floor. The coach who usually had a short fuse controlled himself and reported the incident to me. Mike was removed from the team. I scheduled a meeting with his parents and the meeting started to deteriorate immediately. The father had a pencil and a pad of paper in his hand and appeared to be very angry as a result of the disciplinary action taken by me. He began to cite other instances where boys were playing who were not as good as Mike, although he refused to mention names. The boy's cursing was not a part of his argument. I tried to explain my decision, but it fell on deaf ears. At this point, he told me about another African American player who was not getting playing time. I stopped him in his tracks and bluntly asked if this was a black and white issue, and after hedging somewhat, he said it was. As my blood started to boil, I told him in no uncertain terms that our coaches play the best players and that we were colorblind. I also told him that the Overbrook team that I coached was 90% African American and that I never had any problems in that area. I then got up and told him that the meeting was over and left. Mike was present during this entire exchange and looked somewhat embarrassed. Two days later, Mike, with his head bowed, came into my office and apologized. The JV coach then spoke to him and afterwards recommended that he be reinstated. Subsequently, there was never a behavior problem with him throughout the remainder of the season.

PRACTICE SESSIONS

My frustrations were enormous at this time. I rarely saw any positive changes in the players. The coaches continually barked out the same concerns day after day in the daily practices.

Don't try to make miracle passes—don't telegraph the passes—pass the ball to the pivot man—bounce the pass—lob the pass—the pass is too slow—the pass is too fast—the pass is too low—the pass is too high—don't lead the man too much—hit him on the hands—move the ball from corner to corner—square up—move your feet—slide—guard the base line—keep your hands up—box out—help out on defense—get the ball to the middle man on the fast break—don't cheat on defense—spread the court—

get back on defense—stop standing around—move your feet—drive to the basket—anticipate—keep your rear low to the ground—watch the ball—block the middle—don't rush—shoot the ball—be confident—have courage.

THE LOSSES WERE MOUNTING AGAIN

The feeling of failure was indescribable.

My esteem was terribly low. My mind continued to wander in crooked little corners about misguided decisions, about the possibility of poor judgments about players, and about the abilities or lack of abilities of my players. We lost the last seven games so far in this season and the prospect of winning some future games was very much in doubt. The losses have taken their toll on the players and the coaches. Confidence had all but disappeared. Shooting became strained and easy shots nearly impossible. Everyone was tight and nothing went smoothly. The early enthusiasm of a successful season had turned dramatically into an abyss of pessimism. Tinkering with systems had become commonplace rather than the exception. Seemingly correct decisions today became tomorrow's failures.

After coaching for over twenty years, my confidence about the correctness of putting together all the pieces of a team philosophy had suddenly become unglued. Doubts about my ability continued to consume me. And yet, was I really to blame? Had I misjudged my talent? We were competitive in almost all of the games. The history of the basketball program at this school had been dismal. Why did I think I could change the program when no one really cared and cursory encouragement was the only visible support.

A few years ago, my approach to basketball, as a high school coach, was that I could take any group of players and make winners out of them. That first year at this school proved my assumptions to be correct. With limited ability, we won more games than was predicted. The players on this team started to believe in themselves and their chemistry was great. But, the following years this bubble burst, and I found myself changing my philosophy with the kids. My approach now was to be more patient and, unfortunately, my expectations for success would be measured in smaller clumps. Consistent winning probably would be unreachable and a player's individual progress became the standard. Encouragement and support were the most important factors in helping these young men get through the terrible losses that they would have to endure on many nights. However, they continued to be enthusiastic. They continued to work hard, although I perceived an uncertainty and a lack of confidence that was apparent.

TALK ABOUT BIZARRE

I experienced a really bizarre incident after one game. Jim, who, at times, had dysfunctional moments, got into the game with one minute remaining. We happened to be playing very well, and I was able to get all of the players into the game. Jim was a junior and had some limited potential, and did not get the opportunity to play much. After the game was over, I was standing in the passageway leading to the locker room when Jim came screaming at me and threw his shirt into my face. He yelled in a highly emotional state as he ran into the locker room. He continued his outrage well into the shower room and in front of the astonished players.

I was totally unaware what had occurred or what I could have done. I went into the locker room, very composed, knowing that he was capable of such outbursts. As gently as I could, I asked him what I had done to warrant his rage. Still full of anxiety, he told me that when he entered the game, the announcer introduced him as another player and that I didn't have his name in the book. Fortunately for the team, and me, the announcer erred; otherwise, we would have had a technical assessed to us for an improper lineup. I couldn't appease him. He stomped around, threw his bag down the hallway, and ran out to the bus. He grumbled the entire trip home. The next day in practice, he never even remembered the incident. However, he left the team the next week, and I later learned that he was under psychiatric care.

What compounded the incident even more was that his father came running into the locker room after the game, after all the players had left, screamed, "And the Arabs will get you too!" and ran out of the locker room. I never saw the father again.

WINNING IS A LEARNED EVENT

Winning is a learned event and not something that just happens. What were the things necessary to ensure that victory? Coaches are many times accused of not properly training or, more specifically, not preparing the players correctly so that they can function and perform when the game is on the line.

As usual, this one season again had been a disaster. We normally played well for about thirty out of thirty-two minutes, but when the game was on the line, we collapsed. Here we were playing this last game on the other team's court. The ride alone was an hour up into the country somewhere. Upper Perkiomen, the team that we were playing, was a school with hard-nosed young men from the farm areas. They also were what I call driveway players. Their record over the years paralleled ours, so this was the game of the season. Would we end up in last place or would they? I didn't mind playing a team that was better than we were. My emotions could take that. However, when we played against a team that was poorer than we were, my stomach did tricks on me.

Again, we led until the closing moments. The game was ours until a series of mental blunders occurred that led to our downfall.

Each member of our starting five seemed to contribute in chronological order, starting with our point guard and ending with our center. Here were the events, as I remember them, that led to another heartbreaking loss.

The point guard made an errant unsafe pass that was intercepted. The forward was called for a five second violation, i.e. closely guarded by the opposing player, an open lay-up was missed as was the front end of a one-on-one. The "two guard" was called for traveling and our center was called for a foul, going over the back of an opposing player on the foul line. We lost by six points.

Coaches spend endless hours teaching the players what to do in pressure conditions; however, no one can predict the behavior of a player when the game is on the line. Experience in like situations usually is the best barometer for positive decision-making. The celebration from the other side resembled the winning of the national championship and we then had another long, down-in-the-mouth, ride home.

Bus rides home after losses gave me angina. The junior varsity, which usually never won, laughed, joked, screamed and had a "no effect" mentality. The varsity would not make a sound for fear that the coaches would accuse them of not caring. It took me years just to get them to feel some remorse about losing. When I first took over, the rides home were, on the surface, happier than the ride to the game. It was almost a relief, comic relief, to get it over with.

And each morning, the athletic director who was just doing his job directed me to write a summary of the previous night's game so that it could be announced over the P.A. system. Talk about creativity. I could say anything because nobody ever came to the game, including the newly assigned athletic director. I think he saw four games a year and never a complete game. In fairness, he was assigned athletic responsibilities by the school district although his training was not in the field of athletics. The principal who was a kind, gentle man did care about us, although he was preoccupied with the politics of the school district and his time constraints prohibited him from playing a more active role in the program. He did come to the home games and was a visible supporter.

THE PASSING YEARS

The years passed quietly with few visible changes. The number of wins was always in the single digits. Each year, I was more optimistic than I had a right to be. However, as I have said earlier, coaches are dreamers and we all envision marvelous things when it comes to coaching young men. There were some signs of better athletes and more dedicated basketball players in the high school. Parents were becoming more visibly involved with supportive and positive attitudes. Players wanted to practice more and dedication was on the rise. Players were arriving early and staying long after practice was over.

This new season realistically was one of high hopes. We had some players with experience. Our center was 6'5" tall with long arms and a heart as big as the basketball. Our two guards were nifty ball handlers and our forwards were good shooters and rebounders. We had every reason to be hopeful that this was the season that would turn the program around and erase the memories of the previous years.

Our first important pre-season game was an away game against Upper Dublin, who was coached by Jeff Huddleson. This was a quality suburban school that had a good history of winning games, especially on their home court. We played well throughout the game and the game went into overtime. With ten seconds left, and with the game tied, our best shooting forward was fouled and had two foul shots. Beads of perspiration rolled quickly down from his forehead. The adrenalin raced throughout his body. David's biceps quivered as his sweaty hands gripped the basketball. The home crowd was deathly silent while the opposition screamed obscenities and waved their arms, hoping to distract him. As he stared at the rim, feeling the pressure closing in on him, his thoughts skipped back to the hundreds of practice hours at the foul line. This is what it was all about.

This is what athletes dream about. This was the moment of truth. Two frustrating previous seasons could somewhat be erased with two quick swishes of the net. The coaches and players were frozen, although their hearts were pacing furiously. There had been some previous discussions among the coaches about David's courage in pressure situations, although in practice sessions, this athlete performed beautifully. Mom and Dad, sitting right behind the players' bench couldn't bear to look, their hands tightly clenched together with the blood being squeezed from their fingers. The first shot was over all too quickly. David had been taught to patiently size up the basket, but his anxiety made him rush the shot. It careened off of the front rim. Usually, short shots are caused by tension. The muscles tighten up and the release is not fluid and complete.

Suddenly, the rim looked much smaller. An adjustment had to be made. Be sure that the ball gets over the front part of the rim, but don't over-shoot. Try to concentrate on the shot and not the score. Block out distractions. Concentrate, relax, pray. David stepped off of the foul line and looked to the coaches for encouragement.

The coaches raised their hands with their thumbs up and yelled, "You can do it."

The ball banged off the backboard, hit the rim, and fell hopelessly to the floor as the clock ran out of time. The game went into overtime and ended with the opposition making the winning shot at the buzzer, somewhat foreboding the upcoming season.

We thought that this was going to be the turn around for the team and the program. This picture had been played in my mind over and over so many times in the past, but I thought that this season was a new beginning and things had changed. Despondently, as I walked out to the bus to take another agonizing ride home, I sat with David and tried to console him. I needed to try to get his spirits up as well as the other players. We were all sort of crushed at the loss. We did go on to win ten games that year, although fourteen games were well within our reach.

A TRULY MAGICAL MOMENT

Somewhere near the beginning of this story I told you about the school that pounded us by eighty points and subsequently pounded us each year by large margins. We had never beaten Norristown and never in my wildest dreams could we achieve such a miracle. Here we were, a bunch of typical kids in an affluent suburban community competing against the best players in the state. We were in the second period and losing by about eight points. I was not too uncomfortable. Eight points were not that bad. I could almost live with that kind of spread. But the day before the game, we had been practicing a half-court press with Pete, my six-foot-five center, in the up-front point position of the press. I decided to put the press on, hoping to somehow rattle them.

No one ever dared to press Norristown. Never did their coach expect any such tactic from us. Where did we get the nerve to try such an aggressive strategy against Norristown? And all of a sudden, Pete, my center whose wing span was close to Wilt's, stole the ball from the other team's shifty guard. As the fans silently watched in awe, he swooped down court and exploded to the basket with a thunderous dunk for the first time in his career.

The explosion from the fans was incredible. Suddenly, our team began to play like champions and we won. My point guard, D. J. Johnson, who was going to score 1000 points throughout his career, was fouled at the end of the game and coolly sank both shots. We did the impossible. Everyone was hugging each other after the game. Tears were running down the eyes of our loyal parents.

A FAVOR RETURNED

After many years of frustration, we finally returned the favor to the Norristown coach who had pressed us and embarrassed our team that many years ago. The coach walked away quickly after the game as our fans stood, whistled, cheered, and loudly applauded his departure.

Our teams for the next few years would never be the same. We no longer were the patsies of the league. We now had confidence that we could play against all opposition. Other teams began to look at us with some apprehension instead of just having another easy workout. And coincidentally, we began to get some real ball players who knew how to win.

We wanted to go into the playoffs that year; however, making a decision to go into the playoffs needed the approval of the principal. We did not meet the customary standard of having a winning season although we had a very good one. I was certainly leery of this situation, but I decided to allow the players to talk to the principal, and if they could convince him, then I would move in that direction. The team scheduled a meeting with Mr. Kastle.

The principal's response was:

"When I walked into the hallway outside the locker room after the game on Friday night you (the players) were engaged in discussions with your coaches about the possibility of getting into the state playoffs even though your record did not warrant that position. The guidelines that I have established are clear. But as I listened to your arguments, you offered that you had worked hard all season, that you had improved significantly and now you feel that you are deserving of this opportunity. Normally, I would not have listened to your arguments, but you are not a team of quitters. You have represented our school well. You will most likely encounter a very talented basketball team in the playoffs. Congratulations for being great guys and great representatives of the school district. You won my approval. Good luck in your preparations for the tournament."

We played hard but we were overmatched against Coatesville. They were a superior team that happened to have Richard Hamilton spearheading the team. He now plays for Detroit in the NBA. The inexperience of playing before a few thousand fans unnerved us in the beginning of the game and we fell behind. We were never able to catch up. Our adrenalin did not allow us to execute effectively. We lost by twenty points.

The next day, I wrote a letter to the principal.

Dear Ken,

When we came home from the play-off game last night, the players were in tears hugging each other. The tears were not from the loss, but that the season had ended. I have never coached a group of young athletes such as this group who, in the face of constant adversity, kept their heads about themselves and kept overcoming obstacles all season. They were just incredible. Just to cite a few examples: Alan stood on the sidewalk, outside the gym with tears rolling down his eyes not wanting to go home to an overbearing family. He was just happy to have been a part of the team. Al sat crying in the locker room barely able to get dressed because he knew that his three-year career had ended. Other players, who needed a father image hugged me and would not let go for the longest time.

Although, you had misgivings about the playoffs and the possible pitfalls that might accompany a loss, the excitement generated and the experience of just playing in a meaningful tournament far outweighed the possible negative side effects of a loss. The thrill of just being able to compete and the attempt of winning will never be forgotten by these young impressionable athletes.

It is my wish that an organization of thirty or forty boys and girls could be created to support the basketball teams no matter what the win/loss situation was. Their goal would be to create an atmosphere of enthusiasm and spirit for their peers who were representing the school.

Ken, you and your wife have been there when we needed you and the team and I thank you.

Sincerely,
Coach M

The next year was going to be my last year as a high school coach. Three hundred wins in a long career certainly was a worthy goal and, with luck, I would achieve this goal during the upcoming year.

THE LAST CHAPTER

We finally had the players to make a run for the championship. We had been grooming Richard for two years now. I had not had a young man with so much potential since the Overbrook days. At 6'4, he could dunk the ball with either hand, he was physically strong, and very agile. Blocking shots was what he wanted to do most. I wanted this team to be our shining hour. We had all the parts to complement this guy. D.J. Johnson had already eclipsed the 1,000-point mark. We had speed, balance and rebounding and, most of all, we had experience. We had been grooming some of these players for two years now.

I need to digress and take you back a few years. When Richard was eleven years old, he experienced a situation that traumatized him and continued to haunt him every day of his life.

In 1989, Richard, his brother, and a friend were playing together on a golf course and they came upon a ditch that was filled with what seemed to be casual water. Steve, his friend, waded into this ditch and was immediately sucked down into a drain and disappeared. The boy was later found dead.

Up to this tragic moment, Richard had been an outgoing, good student who had been active in sports and different activities. From that moment on, Richard changed dramatically. He refused to play with friends, he stayed in his house, was lethargic, and his grades suffered dramatically. His friends started to avoid him, and his teacher commented insensitively that, "She gave Richard two weeks to get over his friend's death." For many months, Richard would just sit on his couch and had difficulty breathing. He developed asthma and for short periods of time had trouble breathing. Richard's family transferred him to another school when he was in seventh grade.

His depression continued and he no longer was the good student that he once was. He dropped his old friends, stayed at home playing Nintendo, and did nothing. He became disorganized and lost his lust for life. His grades dramatically suffered in seventh and eighth grades, but he was passed along with the minimal requirements.

Sometime during ninth grade, two additional things happened at home that compounded his psyche. His father, who had some heart problems, had two serious tachycardia attacks that nearly killed him, and his sister announced to the family that she was going to become an unwed mother. During that troubled ninth grade year, Richard had continuous counseling sessions about his bouts with depression concerning that traumatic event. Basketball helped as time went on. Richard seemed to be less depressed and started to play some basketball. In tenth grade, he made the junior varsity basketball team and seemed to be responding well with the companionship of the other players. He still had moments when he became distant, but belonging to a group seemed to help him. He was somewhat more upbeat.

Last year, Richard was in eleventh grade with senior eligibility. Because he repeated ninth grade, he was ineligible to play in his senior year according to the P.I.A.A. rules, unless there were extenuating circumstances.

After discussions with Richard and his parents, I was convinced that we had a shot of gaining eligibility status for an additional season. With the help of the principal, I wrote the following letter to the P.I.A.A., District Chairperson.

Richard is currently in 11th grade with senior eligibility. When he was eleven years old, he experienced a situation that traumatized him and continues to traumatize him every day of his life.

In 1989, Richard, his brother, and a friend were walking together on a golf course and they came upon a ditch that was filled with what seemed to be casual water. His friend, Steve, waded into this ditch and was immediately sucked down into the drain and disappeared. The boy was later found dead.

The letter went on to describe the utter depression that followed Richard's tragic experiences.

Our request was granted. Richard could now play for us in his senior year. He was mandated to take just a few required courses that following year so that his schedule would be light and that he would fulfill the necessary requirements for graduation. All was well for the next basketball season—or was it?

The season started again with high expectations; however, not long into the practice sessions, we noticed that Richard was moody and nonresponsive to the coaches' suggestions and constructive criticisms. It started to become more apparent when he became tired. The psychiatrist informed us that his past was still getting in the way, and that his behavior would remain problematic. His actions vacillated from moment to moment. There were some games that Richard dominated the court by scoring double-digit points as well as double-digit rebounds; there were games that his presence had little effect on the opposition.

In one home game, I substituted for him because he was not productive and as he walked back to the bench, he threw a chair into the aisle next to him, barely missing the principal. I directed my assistant to remove him from the playing floor and escort him to the locker room. When I got there after the game, he was gone.

The next morning, I wrote a report to the athletic director describing the incident. I said in effect that Richard would no longer be a part of the team, since changes in his behavior have not occurred and that he is an embarrassment to the team and to the school.

A few days later, the psychiatrist told me that Richard was now under new medication and that his behavior had been considerably modified informed me.

Would I reconsider my position?

I did, with the principal's approval, and with the proviso that any singular negative behavior would result in dismissal from the team. He responded well and as a team, we now were a force with which to be reckoned. We went on to win many games throughout the middle part of the season without any incidents. We were on a roll until I received word from the school counselor that Richard was flunking wood shop and that the teacher would not budge an inch. I tried talking to the teacher who was a personal friend of mine, but he convinced me that Richard should not receive any additional consideration. He had been a disturbance in the classroom and was given many opportunities to behave. Since he was taking only a few courses, he was now ineligible to compete for the remainder of the season.

I inserted my substitute center into the lineup and we won three of the next six games. Our record was good enough to qualify us for the playoffs.

We played against Conestoga, one of the co-champions of the Central league, on their home court and we won in overtime. This was another victory that remains with me forever. This is the school district where I had been the principal for fifteen years and to return "home" to win our program's first ever post-season game was as rewarding to me as Overbrook's City Championships of the 1950s.

I remember looking into the stands and on the top

row was that small group of hostile faculty members sitting and just staring down at my team and me.

My former assistant principal, Dave Cowburn, who was with me for fifteen years at my junior high was now working at Conestoga High as the athletic director.

He just looked at me and smiled.

REFLECTIONS

Al Perlini 1990–1993 *William Tennent*

I wanted to be a professional basketball player. My parents sent me to two basketball camps each summer. One would be an overnight camp with Rollie Massamino and the other at Jay Wright's camp in Southhampton when he was an assistant at Villanova. I loved it.

I was in ninth grade and this grade was still in junior high school. I was selected as the M.V.P. player on the ninth grade team, and I just couldn't wait to meet you since your reputation as a basketball coach at Overbrook and Upper Moreland preceded you. During the summer in my sophomore year, you invited me to play with the varsity in the summer league. You were right. The mentality in the city is much different than in the suburbs. It's like apples and oranges. The city players are so dedicated that they play basketball 24/7.

I got into a dozen or so games that summer and held my own. I was a starter now because of the poor turnout from my soon-to-be teammates who were leftovers from last year. By the end of the summer, my game had improved dramatically, and I was excited about the upcoming season. I worked out every day in September and October, and I very clearly remember you saying to me that I was a "gym rat" and that's great. I knew that you liked dedication and, at this early age, I did not want to disappoint you. In this league, a player could only play a total of four quarters on a given night, and you clearly told me that I would play three quarters for the junior varsity and sit on the varsity bench for 1 quarter. I really didn't care much about the junior varsity. All I cared about was the varsity. My dad was a great cheerleader and started the William Tennent Boosters' club. He wanted to generate support from the parents. He wanted us to be a family. He wanted us to look good, to have sweaters, and have spirit like the "Hoosiers." I got into a few games that season and scored ten points all season. However in the spring of 1991, my biggest supporter, my dad, developed a brain aneurysm and died.

At that point, I dedicated my life to my dad. I felt like I went from a boy to a man very quickly.

The summer of my junior year, our school hosted a summer league for the first time. My dad always thought that we should do something to promote basketball at the school and raise money at the same time for the program. The school had beautiful facilities and only later, playing in college, did I realize that Tennent had better accommodations that some division II and III schools. That summer, we struggled with our identity. The season that followed was totally dysfunctional. I started the first game because one of the starting forwards was hurt. We lost by twenty-five points. However, I scored twenty-one points and pulled down fifteen rebounds. You told me that the team was going to need all of my skills this coming year. The season was a real eye-opening experience. The seniors were not performing at all and after six games, three of them quit the team with support from their parents. I played every game and, at the end of the season, I was selected All League Second Team. We were losing many games, my dad was gone, and all I could think about was how and when we were going to start to win. The bus rides home were painful. A handful of players did not seem to care. In fact, I stood up and yelled at them for not caring.

I really don't know how I was selected for this award on a team with such a terrible losing record. My passion propelled me forward in my senior year. For me, preparation was key. I would have a pre-game meal and a shower before the game as if I had a Friday night date.

My date was with a basketball on a basketball court somewhere in Delaware County. If we lost, I would be the last guy out of the locker room, and you would talk to me for what seemed like hours about the game. And when I got home, my mom would talk to me for more hours after a tough loss.

Finally, my season and career were coming to an end. I remember my last regular season game. The day was endless. I didn't want the night to arrive because it was going to be over too fast, and I wasn't sure if I would ever play in college. That night was Senior Night and the seniors were being honored with their parents. However, I was emotionally torn because my dad wasn't there to be proud of me.

After the game, I just sat there and cried. I knew that an important part of my life was over. And as I reflect, I loved every minute of it.

The wins were few and far between, but I learned about life from you, my coach, and about persevering through emotional heartaches throughout the three seasons that we had together.

I was a walk-on at Saint Joseph's College after high school, and I was a part of that basketball program for two years before Coach Griffin resigned at the end of my sophomore year.

I will never forget the years I spent with you and the lessons that you taught me, and the sheer excitement when we upset a few teams.

Thank you for everything and especially for your caring.

—Al Perlini

RELECTIONS

Dear Mr. M,

Thank you for your care and coaching that you gave to our son, Bob. Under your guidance and coaching, Bob developed a true love for basketball. None of his friends who played basketball in high school have stuck it out in college. He is attending Grove City College and has finally made the varsity. It hasn't been easy, but he is hoping that you are proud of him.

You brought him on carefully and never threw him to the wolves. When he was ready, you gave him his opportunity and he did well. You gave him the confidence to play college ball and we thank you for that. As a result of basketball, his confidence has grown and helped him mature as a young man. How do we thank you for your love of our son? We cannot thank you enough. You were always there for him and always a gentleman and a friend to Bob. We will never forget the lessons that you taught him.

Thank you again, coach, for coaching our son. You have affected so many young men's lives in a positive way, so please retire with many good memories of basketball.

Sincerely,

Bob and Claire Ayton, Parents, William Tennent

PART VI—THE COMMUNITY COLLEGE OF PHILADELPHIA

I have taught part-time as an instructor in the Community College of Philadelphia in a program called Adult Basic Education since 1990. The individual rewards of this program are as great as winning basketball games. Since I always wanted to work with young people, this was a wonderful opportunity to fill my time each morning, waiting to coach in the afternoon. Little did I know that the intrinsic rewards would be so rewarding. My college students over the years have been young and middle-aged inner city people who are looking to improve their status in life. They are self-motivated to achieve goals that may, for some, be unachievable, but there have been many individual successes of the students that a few years ago were unimaginable and unthinkable. Coming from backgrounds that included poverty, drugs, unwanted pregnancies, and tragedies, they want to better their lives with promises that their futures will be improved. The students' goals are lofty. They are trying to become nurses, business people, educators, and even criminologists. For the most part, their educational backgrounds are horrific, but they are determined to succeed and their perseverance is beyond belief. This program basically provides an opportunity to learn to speak and write better with an emphasis on correct grammar, vocabulary building, and reading comprehension. My goal in these classes is to get the students to pass the placement test of the college. Many of them originally failed the test and are trying to improve their skills to retake the test after my class. But what has astounded me is the confidence that these students have developed. They seem to stand taller, speak with confidence, and are not afraid to voice their opinions. I don't give grades. They are told that they will achieve their goals through effort and perseverance.

Angel, who was my student for six consecutive semesters, wrote the following letter when he finally passed his placement test.

"My name is Angel Gonzales and I have been out of school for twenty-four years. I have seven children and I operate a pizza shop before and after the class. Since returning to school, I have learned a great deal. With Mr. M's expertise in teaching and his generous involvement in helping each and everyone of the students in his class, I have been able to pass my placement test and my thanks to him from the bottom of my heart. This has raised my level of confidence beyond my imagination."

I have had students from Haiti, China, South and West Africa, Jamaica, and, of course, the inner city of Philadelphia. One of my students, who was with me for three semesters, was caught in the civil war in Africa and had his right arm severed with a machete. He learned to write with his left hand and when he finally passed his placement test, he told me that he wanted to become a lawyer and go back to Africa to help his nation. I was told that he was doing well in his classes and that it appeared that he was going to achieve his goals. Those are just two success stories about my students, but I could have mentioned hundreds of other stories. The one story that follows will remain with me forever.

Roberta was a pleasant, upbeat, always smiling seventy-two-year-old African-American woman who continually came to my class so that she could eventually get a high school diploma. She only went to the fifth grade when she lived in the South. She desperately wanted the diploma so that she could help young folks as they were growing up. This was her prize. This was her remaining ultimate goal. She was very diligent and conscientious, but it was doubtful that she was ever going to accomplish her goal. One day, she didn't show up for class and I asked her sister-in-law where she was because she never missed a class. With tears in her eyes, she told me that Roberta had had a stroke and was in the

University of Penn Hospital. The prognosis was not very good.

I was able to contact the Department of Education in Harrisburg and we were able to devise a certificate that simulated a diploma, spelling out her achievements in the community and in her class. I presented her with the certificate in the hospital room with her family present and with photographers from the local newspapers. She couldn't speak, but the tears rolled down her face as she hugged the certificate and me.

She died the next day.

How does one describe the emotions that accompany this sadness? She is like the thousands of adult students who frequent these classes throughout the country attempting to make their lives a little bit better.

And then each day, after my morning classes, I prepared myself mentally for the difficult afternoon basketball sessions.

PART VII—Retirement

I thought that I was going to retire the following year after fifty years in basketball and education. It was time for me to go. But two more opportunities surfaced that I couldn't turn down. I was asked to coach a Maccabi/United States team of 14, 15, and 16-year-old basketball players who were from all over the country. We would be playing in the European games in Sterling, Scotland, against many European countries including Georgia, (Russia), England, Switzerland. The competition was intense and everyone wanted to beat the U.S. but their skills didn't match the American team. Going undefeated and winning by large margins, our team breezed through the competition and was awarded the championship Gold Medal. I couldn't have been prouder when we walked into the stadium during the closing ceremonies carrying the American flag and hearing the national anthem.

The second opportunity came about when a Daily News reporter was interviewing me and asked me if I was ever going to coach again. With tongue in cheek, I said that I would like to coach ninth grade girls. Little did I know that he was going to put that statement in the newspaper article that he was writing. The next day, Barry Kirsch, the girls' basketball coach from Archbishop Carroll called me and asked me if I would coach his ninth grade girls at Archbishop Carroll in the Catholic league. I knew of Barry's reputation as a fine coach and a wonderful gentleman and I immediately said "yes" and I coached there for six years. The girls were wonderful and responsive for all that we tried to do for them and we were very successful; however, girls are far different than coaching boys.

Our teams usually lost only one or two games a season in those six years and the girls responded to everything we tried to teach them except I lost their concentration when a boy entered the gym. All eyes shifted from me to the other side of the gym where the boy was standing, and then they sheepishly looked back at me as I waited for their attention. After one of the games, Bridgett asked me, "How did I do?" I responded as gently as I could that she played well, but she only shot one for twelve. She quickly responded, "Well, I can't make every shot."

I must tell the reader one classic story about

ninth grade girls that has everyone laughing who hears it.

We were playing an important game and the score was very close with a few minutes to play. I wanted to get Heather into the game and I called her over to me from the bench and told her that she was going in for Kelly and that we were playing "man to man." She needed to ask Kelly whom she was guarding because it was very important that she knew what to do. She turned to me and with a straight, serious look in her face said, "I'm not talking to Kelly." I looked at my assistant coach, Aaron Bitman, who dropped his head and would not even look at me. I looked into the stands, and my friends who heard the conversation were convulsed with laughter. That story brings bursts of laughter from everyone who hears it.

I received many wonderful letters when I left coaching. I have included a few of the memorable ones from special coaches and parents. The first one is special since it came from one of my players from the Overbrook era of fifty years ago He was the shooting guard on the first team that I ever coached at Overbrook.

Dear Coach,

On behalf of all the players, we congratulate you for achieving a coaching career that spans many decades. After fifty years, the legendary coach is still spoken of with praise.

There's no doubt that you had what it takes to become a basketball star and when the sneakers were hung up, the passion, skills, and knowledge of the game were passed on to others under your care.

Now that the whistle and chalkboard are stashed away, please be assured that there is a "basketball heaven" for those who ate, slept, and drank basketball.

During the twilight of our years, when memories pop up more and more, the name of Cecil Mosenson will come to mind and the corollary: man, hero, super coach.

Godspeed,

Doug Leaman.

March, 1999

Dear Coach,

I understand that you are retiring from coaching at William Tennent. I'd like to wish you the best in your future. It was always a challenge to prepare for a game with your team. Even when you didn't have much talent, you always found a way to stay in the game. You certainly have had a good effect on the William Tennent basketball program. The athletes have been fortunate to have learned from you because you taught them to give 100 percent.

I really don't know who can take your place, but they certainly will have a tough act to follow. It has been a pleasure knowing you,

Sincerely,
Sheldon Per
Coach
Bensalem High School

Feb 20, 1998
Dear Coach,

Congratulations for the outstanding coaching career.

Winning more that 300 games is the envy of every coach in the profession and you did it even though you were a principal for fifteen years and out of coaching during that time.

You are a credit to the schools where you have coached and the players you have been associated with during your career. I have enjoyed sitting with you and talking to you before our games.

The respect and admiration shown to you by your student athletes have always been admirable. You were able to develop the "will to win" and the sportsmanship so necessary for their adult success.

Thank you for the integrity and the

devotion that has been so evident throughout your career.

Sincerely,

Robert Hart

Athletic Director

Bensalem School district

AWARDS

- Coach of the Year—Temple University 1955
- Coach of the Year—Buxmont League 1964
- National Award For Excellence in Education –President Ronald Reagan 1987
- Springfield, Massachusetts. Basketball Hall of Fame 1990
- Jewish Basketball League Alumni Awards 1982, 1998, 2005
- Overbrook Hall of Fame 2007
- Philadelphia Jewish Sports Hall of Fame 2007

This picture represents my retirement from coaching. The players are from two eras. Upper Moreland and William Tennent.

Retirement Award From Previous Players
Left to right: Joe Vesey, Al Perlini, John Faulkner,
Joe Faulkner, Hank Faulkner

Cecil and Joan
European Maccabi Games United States
Gold Medal Ceremony, Scotland, 1999

**1999 European Games
Gold Medal Winners**

Girls Basketball Team
Archbishop Carroll Girls Team 2002–2003
Front Row: Colleen McGee, Catherine Gallagher, Megan Redding,
Megan Brennan. Second Row: Vanessa Coll, Collette Guifalco,
Colleen Defruscio, Kathleen Kenny. Third Row: Coach Aaron
Bitman Kelly Bosco, Jamie Esbensen, Alicia Vasssalo
Coach Cecil Mosenson

SUMMARY

I constantly think about my career that was filled with a lifetime of memories. I started with a dream team, moved on to a wonderful fifteen years at Upper Moreland High School, coaching wonderful young people. Then, becoming a principal in an upscale school district, moving on to coach at William Tennent and at Archbishop Carroll, and ending knowing that I helped thousands of young people in and out of basketball to become productive and contributing citizens in our society.

There is not a week that passes where I do not drift back to recall the great Wilt or recall developing less talented players and getting the same joy from these players as I got from my Overbrook years.

The awards I have received throughout my career have been warmly accepted, but I just can't say enough about the people who helped me achieve at such levels.

I will miss the excitement, but mostly, I will miss the hundreds of youngsters whom I have personally touched for half a century. The wonderful feeling of seeing my athletes and students succeed in our society and the hundreds of notes and letters that I have received over these many years have made me feel that my contributions have far exceeded my expectations.

My wonderful wife and my three sons, who always patted me on the back during difficult times, were always with me as I moved onward in my life's work.

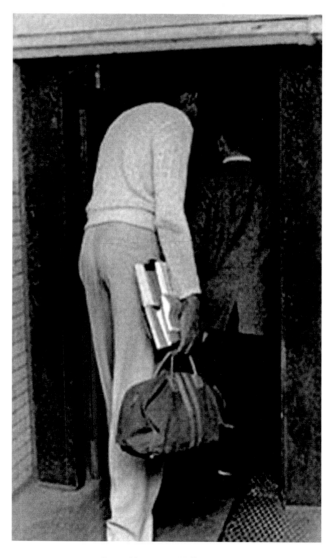

**Goodbye and Thank You
Wilt and Coach**

It was a great ride.
I am so grateful to have had the wonderful
opportunities that were offered to me. I thank my
family, my dear friends, my players, and my students
for allowing me to be a part of their lives
and to have served them for over 50 years.

Biography

Cecil Mosenson was born in West Philadelphia on December 11, 1929. He attended Overbrook High School and played basketball there on an undefeated team. He received a basketball scholarship to Temple University and after college played against the Harlem Globetrotters with the Washington Generals. He also played in the Eastern Professional Basketball League. At the age of 22, he was appointed the head basketball coach of Overbrook High School where he inherited the basketball star Wilt Chamberlain. He went on to teach and coach at a suburban high school and then was appointed principal at Tredyffrin/Easttown Junior High School in Berwyn, Pa. During his tenure there, his school was selected by the United States Department of Education as one of the top junior highs in the country and he was honored in the Rose Garden by President Ronald Reagan. He currently teaches in the community college of Philadelphia. He has received numerous basketball coaching honors throughout his career.

Index of Names